22: PERSPECTIVES IN CRITICISM

PERSPECTIVES IN CRITICISM

22:

H. PORTER ABBOTT

The Fiction of Samuel Beckett

Form and Effect

UNIVERSITY OF CALIFORNIA PRESS

Berkeley   Los Angeles   London

1973

ISBN: 0-520-02202-5
LIBRARY OF CONGRESS CATALOG CARD NO.: 79-186102
Printed in the United States of America

For Anita

Acknowledgments

I WISH TO record my gratitude to the following:

Professor Hugh Kenner, for placing at my disposal a typescript of *Mercier et Camier* and a photograph copy of *More Pricks Than Kicks* and for making certain shrewd suggestions about the appropriate disposition of my material.

Professors John Carroll, Melvin J. Friedman, David Gordon, and Edgar Bowers, for help and encouragement.

Peter Janke, for typing a superb copy of the manuscript and for going over my translations of Beckett's French which appear in chapter four.

Richard and Christine Helgerson, for going over those same translations.

The Secretarial staff of the English Department at the University of California, Santa Barbara, for typing successive drafts of the manuscript.

The Academic Senate of the University of California, Santa Barbara, for a General Research Grant to help in the preparation of the manuscript.

University of Wisconsin Press, for allowing the republication of much of the material from my article "Farewell to Incompetence: Beckett's *How It Is* and *Imagination Dead Imagine*," (*Contemporary Literature*, vol. XI, no. 1, [© 1970 by the Regents of the University of Wisconsin], pp. 36–47), which appears in chapter eight of this volume.

Grove Press for permission to quote from *How It Is*

(copyright © 1964 by Grove Press), *Murphy, Proust, Stories and Texts for Nothing* (copyright © 1967 by Samuel Beckett), *Three Novels* (copyright © 1955, 1956, 1958, by Grove Press), and *Watt*.

Les Éditions de Minuit, for permission to quote from *Mercier et Camier* (copyright © 1970 by Les Éditions de Minuit).

My wife, Anita, for close reading and good advice.

H. P. A.

Santa Barbara

Contents

Introduction

THE MAIN PURPOSE of this book is to show how, in the fiction he wrote between 1940 and 1959, Beckett experimented with what Yvor Winters called "imitative form," and to develop a mode of critical response which is appropriate to that experiment. This also provides a way of understanding the work that appeared immediately after in the 1960s as well as the apprenticeship Beckett underwent in the 1930s. This study does not pretend to be comprehensive, or exclusive. It is of form, but not formalist. It is also a version of what has come to be called, somewhat ambiguously, "affective criticism" insofar as it examines form in terms of its effect on the reader. This is essentially a matter of emphasis. Form in Beckett has commonly been examined in terms of its relationship to the author, or in terms of the increasing anxiety of that relationship. Beckett has often appeared, in consequence, as very closely identifiable with his creations (Beckett-Watt becoming Beckett-Molloy), involved in their quest, and at the same time trapped, as they are, in an inevitable process of fictional disintegration. My stress is on Beckett the craftsman, disengaged from his characters, seeking not to undertake but to present their quest. By the time he wrote *Watt,* Beckett had become a cunning literary strategist who wrote with an acute awareness of the effect his fiction had on its audience.

There are two extremes in Beckett criticism. One reads Beckett as an allegorist who reveals certain awe-

1

some paradoxes about life. The other reads him as the allegorist's literary alter ego, a kind of *symboliste* who happens to use certain paradoxes in order to create brilliant formal events. If the two were to debate, however, it would be the critic of pure form who would have most of the arguments. He would be emphasizing, to begin with, that Beckett after all is not a philosopher but an artist. In addition, he would have Beckett's own spare comments on art to assist him. In 1945, for example, Beckett dedicated an essay on the painters Abraham and Gerardus van Velde to "l'inoffensif loufouque qui court, comme d'autres au cinéma, dans les galeries, au musée et jusque dans les églises avec l'espoir—tenez-vous bien—de jouir. Il ne veut pas s'instruire, le cochon, ni devenir meilleur. Il ne pense qu'á son plaisir." [1] Better known is the reply to the critics lodged in *Happy Days:*

> And at last this man Shower—or Cooker—ends in er anyway—stake my life on that—What's she doing? he says—What's the idea? he says—stuck up to her diddies in the bleeding ground—coarse fellow—What does it mean? he says—What's it meant to mean?—and so on—lot more stuff like that—usual drivel—Do you hear me? he says—I do, she says, God help me—What do you mean, he says, God help you? . . . And you, she says, what's the idea of you, she says, What are you meant to mean? [2]

"I don't know what his plays are about," Brendan Behan once said, "but I do know I enjoy them. I do not know what a swim in the ocean is about, but I enjoy it. I enjoy the water flowing over me." [3] Implicit here is the rejection of criticism altogether. The compromise is, at least, to reject "interpretation" and follow the course advocated by Susan Sontag, "to show *how it is what it is,* even *that it is what it is,* rather than to show *what it means."* [4] As John Fletcher remarked in 1966, "Beckett's extraordinary power cannot lie in what he says, and so it must lie in the way he says it." [5]

But Beckett is not solely concerned with the *way* he says what he says. If he is a "formalist," he is nonetheless involved in what can still be described as an imitation of life; and it is the life that finally determines the way he composes. The point is at once obvious and tricky, but it is an important point and can be amplified with profit by going back to Beckett's essay on Proust (1931), an exercise in which Beckett is clearly developing his own aesthetic ideas as well as writing about Proust. In it Beckett develops certain postulates, not simply about aesthetic experience but about the nature of all experience. These can be summarized briefly as follows.

Without lasting perceptions of order, men are afflicted with a feeling of insecurity—an agony. Most men are endowed with two highly developed faculties —Memory and Habit—which enable them to perceive order and hence to achieve security. Memory and Habit tie past, present, and future together, allow a life to be abstracted from flux, imply causality and development. The "higher" constructs, too, arise from Memory and Habit: schemes of history, philosophies, psychologies, moralities. All these are myths generated by man's need for security. There are a few men, however, who have a need for demythologized experience. They are willing to undergo the agony of insecurity for a perception of things as they are and an experience of time as it is, unmanacled from Memory and Habit. Such perceptive experiences Beckett labels alternatively "new" or "true" experiences. They are always unique, even though they may be remembered (not to be confused with elements of Memory which, being ever present, are never remembered). What is experienced will not yield to rational examination, indeed "the essence of any new experience is contained precisely in

3

[the] mysterious element." [6] It is immediate, particular, affective, and as enchanting as it is agonizing.

The point to stress is that what Beckett says about the beauty of the unattached object and the new or true experience leads directly to what he says about art: "Hamm as stated, and Clov as stated, together as stated, nec tecum nec sine te, in such a place, and in such a world, that's all I can manage, more than I could." [7] The classical artist who "assumes omniscience and omnipotence" and who "raises himself artificially out of Time in order to give relief to his chronology and causality to his development" [8] is the artist of Habit and Memory. The romantic, like Proust or Beckett, is the artist of "true" experience. He assumes impotence, not omnipotence, and opposes "the particular affective evidential state to all the subleties of rational cross-reference." [9] The true experience is, as it were, the source and end and test of art. If Beckett is successful, he generates in us the kinds of agony and enchantment that attend any true perception of things as they are. He attempts to bring us back to the unfettered experience of the world. And thus, to return to our original concern, what is needed is a critical method that will avoid so strict a formalism that this content, if you will, is unduly neglected.

Between allegory and pure formalism is an approach epitomized in the recent and remarkable study by Olga Bernal, *Langage et fiction dans le roman de Beckett.* It examines Beckett's canon as its own dilemma: a literature founded on the impossibility of representation and the disengagement of language from the world. As the author points out, the dilemma is the critic's as well:

> La position du critique reflète, elle aussi, le dilemme de l'art moderne qui est celui de la représentation. En face de cet art, aucun critique ne s'enquiert du "contenu" d'une oeuvre. S'il est tenté de poser la question: "de quoi y a-t-il représenta-

tion?", il ne la formule pas. Cette question tradi-
tionelle est en fait désuète puisque le "quoi" n'est
plus au coeur de l'oeuvre. Ce qui y est, c'est la
déstructure du "quoi." [10]

Yet, as I read this, the destruction of the "what" becomes itself a "what," communicated to, digested, and
often ingeniously expounded by Professor Bernal. Her
book is an implicit assertion of its existence. Without a
"what," criticism becomes a sustained suspension of
disbelief. Similarly, the act of writing, or at least publication, is predicated on the assumption that some relation exists between the reader and the book—a relation, moreover, which can be controlled at least to
some extent by the author.

Beckett, to be sure, is responsible for much uncertainty on this subject: uncertainty that he nourishes
almost coquettishly. Thus, in his famous dialogues with
Duthuit (1949), he asserts that there is no relation
whatsoever between a work of art and its "occasion" and
scrupulously protects his assertion by claiming that
this absence itself—which means, in effect, the impossibility of expression—is likewise inexpressible. Yet he
asserts this in the context of defining an art that is
the expression that there is nothing to express," and
so on (italics mine).

No, no, allow me to expire. I know that all that
is required now, in order to bring even this hor-
rible matter to an acceptable conclusion, is to
make of this submission, this admission, this fidel-
ity to failure, a new occasion, a new term of relation, and of the act which, unable to act, obliged
to act, he makes, an expressive act, even if only
of itself, of its impossibility, of its obligation. I
know that my inability to do so places myself, and
perhaps an innocent, in what I think is still called
an unenviable situation, familiar to psychiatrists.[11]

5

To respond properly to these dialogues it is necessary to recognize what kind of a critic Beckett has become since his essay on Proust. As Beckett said himself: "It is impossible for me to talk about my writing because I am constantly working in the dark. It would be like an insect leaving his cocoon. I can only estimate my work from within." [12] This, I think, accounts for the highly elaborate dance with Duthuit. Beckett, in other words, is not so much talking about his art here as he is performing it. Insofar as it is commentary, it is an estimate "from within." But, as critics, we do not share Beckett's self-imposed limitations. Unless we are to throw over our vocation, we must necessarily talk from a vantage point outside art. Thus, to begin with this dialogue, it is possible for us to affirm that through the author's straining and convoluted rhetoric we experience something of the expressive disaster that is his occasion.

What I have just performed on the dialogue is a very elementary example of the critical approach adopted in this study for Beckett's work from *Watt* to *Texts for Nothing*. It involves essentially what can be called a response to "imitative form." The phrase "imitative" or "expressive form" comes, without his pejorative connotations, from Yvor Winters who defined it as the attempt to "imitate the subject in the form" of a work of art. Winters actually used the phrase interchangeably for two rather different concepts. One is a concept of the genesis of art, expressed in Winters characteristically as the notion that "Form is expressive invariably of the state of mind of the author." [13] This is the D. H. Lawrence theory of poetic expression which R. P. Blackmur defined as "the faith . . . that if a thing is only intensely enough felt its mere expression in words will give it satisfactory form, the dogma, in short, that once material becomes words it is its own best form." [14] At the lowest level this is automatic writing, and Beckett to my knowledge has never practiced it. The other con-

6

cept, the one we are interested in, is a concept of imitation. In Winters it appears in such statements as "the form of expression is determined by the subject matter" or the attempt "to imitate the subject in the form of a work of art." This is quite different from the other concept. It starts with a belief about the way form takes part in imitation rather than the way it comes into being: specifically, it assumes that form is, or can be, imitative.[15]

As a critical method, what this means is that we understand the work not only through what it says but through how it says it. In the context of the debate between the allegorist and the formalist, the point to stress is that we *do* have an understanding. It in turn is something we can talk about in relation to the form that produces it. It provides a way of controlling discussion of form.

The term "content"—associated as it is with some package of abstractions, some message—is perhaps an inadequate term to designate this understanding. Though Beckett is a mimetic artist, his content, like his occasion, is neither an empirical Balzacian universe nor a set of philosophic truths. It is the immediate experience of a variety of mysteries. Thus, when we speak of "imitation" we refer not so much to a notion of reflection or representation as we do to a generation in the reader of experiences that are at the same time the subject of the work. Through imitative form, in other words, the reader is forced into a relationship with the book, which imitates the central figure's relationship with his world. There ought, perhaps, to be a bettter term than "imitative form," but in its absence it is important to stress this version of "imitation." The procedure admits of a much more extensive and various working of form than the simple representational mode of the shape poem (or the shapeless one: Beckett's method is rarely so badly iconic as, say, Whitman's baggy figuring of America). His work is at once about

7

and creative of what Beckett called "true experience." And his double ends are effected through the subtle manipulation of a host of formal components: the archetypal pattern, the narrator, the report, the two-part form, storytelling, the tale of espionage, syntax.

That Beckett employed imitative form is no great discovery. It is essentially the basis of Martin Esslin's distinction between the Theatre of the Absurd and the drama of Camus and Sartre. In discussion of Beckett's drama, at least, the notion of imitative form, though not explicitly described as such, has gained a certain acceptance and has yielded some excellent commentary. Lawrence Harvey, for example, has shown how Beckett develops the Berkeleyan theme, *esse est percipi*, through a constant and varied manipulation of metaphors—like audience and actors—which are built into the performed play.[16]

In criticism of the fiction, however, the concept of imitative form has never been reflected in any consistent critical method. This quite probably stems from the fact that it is much easier to apply the concept to drama because of the nature of the medium. Criticism of imitative form leads to a kind of analysis that deals with what could be called the "immediate experience" of a work. And it is far easier to speak of the stage in terms of immediate experience and to equate that experience with the subject of the play, than it is of fiction. Fictional experience is more reflective. One has no physical presences. One is not trapped in a room and forced to undergo an experience. One can put the book down, think about it, look up words. And as one does so, the book changes. It is harder to conceive of in terms of immediate experience. Yet, immediacy is one of the basic features of "true experience" and became a dominating formal concern in Beckett's fiction for two crucial decades.

What this formal experimentation requires from the critic is to find ways of talking about Beckett's fiction

8

as an imitation of life without producing those often elaborate structures of meaning, knit from a variety of "clues," which have marred so many otherwise excellent discussions of Beckett. Part of the problem is learning how to exercise the proper amount of restraint. We can acknowledge the virtue of concentrating on immediate effect, perhaps even "simply responding" to a Beckett piece, knowing that there are no keys, heeding the author's warning not to "have headaches among the overtones." [17] Yet we cannot avoid noticing that there are "overtones" and certainly many elements that at least appear to be keys. Thus Beckett drives many of his critics to allegory, even though allegory is the kind of coherence he has striven to avoid. One must accept Beckett's "keys" in the spirit in which they are given. It is perfectly in order for the reader of *Molloy* to see Gabriel in Gaber and Yahweh in Youdi so long as he does not get a headache trying to establish that Youdi *is* Yahweh and that the rest of the book conforms with such an interpretation. Youdi is like Yahweh but Youdi is still Youdi.

Let us look at two examples, one from the plays and one from the fiction, to show the appropriateness of this kind of tact to both genres. Observe, to begin with, what an ingenious mind can do with "the picture turned to the wall" in *Endgame:*

> Someone is in disgrace, has disgraced those left behind. The suggestion is too salient for Beckett not to have meant us to make something of it. But who is out of grace? All of us, none of us? What pictures, turned to the wall, would mean either of these? It is possible we are to be left guessing, like his characters. I have imagined it variously: as an illustration of a biblical scene (perhaps of the creation); as an icon portrait of Christ; as a family portrait of the four characters. It now seems to me that the picture may be turned not because

9

anyone special is in disgrace, nor everyone special, but just because it is a picture. It is art itself which is disgraced, cursed because it makes the artist special, bullies his audience into suffering for him, contains his meaning, tells stories, loves floods.[18]

This is intriguing, but the very abundance of possibilities underlines the gratuitousness of the conclusion. One could take any one of Mr. Cavell's "guesses" and erect upon it an interpretation, but he is closest to the truth when he says: "It is possible we are to be left guessing." Yet why should we even guess? If our guessing could get us anywhere, Beckett would have provided a way accessible to more than one or two detectives. As Beckett replied to those who sought the identity of Godot: "If I knew, I would have said so in the play." [19]

What Beckett has done in this instance is really quite clear. He has communicated concealment. Just as Godot is important not because of who he is but because he is not present, so the picture derives its importance not because of what it represents but because it cannot be seen. This is its immediate effect. A picture is turned to the wall. We begin and end with that fact. Such an interpretation may come as a dull thud, but it is the best description of what happens in the play. Concealment, or conversely blindness, is one of the things the play is very much about. And we are put in the same situation as the characters. We experience not-knowing. We cannot see the world outside, we cannot see the lower regions of Nag and Nell, we cannot see the future or the past.

To illustrate the same approach in fiction, let us look at the names of two mysterious figures in *Molloy*: A and C. In the original French, Molloy called them A and B, which in a way makes it even more tantalizing that in the English we are faced with A and C. It is not surprising that these two figures have been variously interpreted as, for example, Cain and Abel; Mercier and Camier; the two thieves, one damned and one saved, who represent so well for Beckett the mysteries of cosmic dispensation; Art and Con, the twin dwarfs in *Watt*, revived as a faint reminder of the earlier work; and even Alternating Current, since A is coming and C is going and, as we know, all experience is flux.

Some of these explanations are more tenable than others. But, granting the possibility of a far better hypothesis than any listed above, the quest for it nonetheless leads us away from the value of A and C. For the value of A and C lies mainly in the absence of B. The beauty lies in the absence of explanation. It is a remarkable commentary on the mind that chose so to enumerate these two figures, and it is quite funny. The reader who laughs at this experiences an enchantment that the man with the explanation may have deprived himself of, at the expense of time and considerable effort. This is not to say that we murder to dissect. Prolonged analysis after reading does not have to mutilate the effect of rereading. But it is necessary that the conclusion arrived at not interfere with the effect we have been discussing: an effect that bears more weight in Beckett's fiction than it does in the fiction of almost any other serious writer.

There is one more point that needs mentioning before we turn to the works themselves. A theorist of imitative form might argue that all literary forms are imitative, that, in other words, the plot with beginning, middle, and end, or the iambic pentameter line are forms which in themselves are expressive, whether the author realizes it or not. Such a view would imply that all authors are inevitably practitioners of imitative form. Whether or not this is true, it does appear that the *conscious* application of the method occurs most frequently in the work of artists who are primarily concerned with imitating the absurd, the irrational, or the mysterious, and consequently who follow the logic of the theory and reject the conventions of their rationalist forebears. Thus the case that Martin Esslin, as well as Robbe-Grillet and Sarraute, made against Camus and Sartre was that Camus and Sartre expressed their "absurdist" views in "non-absurdist" conventions. "If Camus argues that in our disillusioned age the world has ceased to make sense, he does so in the elegantly rationalistic and discursive style of an eighteenth-century moralist, in well-constructed and polished plays." [20] Winters also found that the conscious practitioners of imitative form were those who wished to imitate a reality that was essentially disordered.

It should be noted before continuing with this point that "disorder" is a compromise term, tepid and somewhat misleading. The logical term to use would be "chaos," especially because Beckett has used it himself. I hesitate to do so, however, because chaos—like other popular terms that have been applied to Beckett's subject: void, nought, zero—strikes me as unutterably dull and in no way suggestive of that enchantment one experiences in reading Beckett. Furthermore, Beckett is too much of a skeptic to assert the existence of chaos. His occasion is an experience, not a fact; and the experience is one of not-knowing. Thus it contains no single unambiguous quality and must even be complicated by a sense of order. There is nothing mysterious about an undifferentiated plenum. "If there were only darkness," Beckett is reported to have said, "all would be clear. It is because there is not only darkness but also light that our situation becomes inexplicable." [21]

To return to our subject, what I find most interesting is the conjunction of the two notions, form and disorder, or form and chaos. For the use of imitative form, at least, to express disorder is logically a contradiction in terms. It is hard to conceive of form as anything else but a kind of order. Correlatively, the formal imita-

12

tion of disorder would appear to reach its logical re-
duction in the elimination of form altogether. There is
a law of diminishing returns. Ultra Violet, one of Andy
Warhol's leading ladies recently defended her director
by stating that "sometimes in Andy's movies nothing
happens, and that's good because in life sometimes
nothing happens—and you should see reality on the
screen." [22] Ultra Violet got the message, of course, but
anyone who has endured certain portions of a Warhol
film may find the message small compensation for
the effort involved. It is a short step from this to the
abandonment of art altogether, because the ultimate in
imitative form is the thing itself. One follows the same
route as Swift's projectors at the Academy of Lagado
who, in the interests of precision, rejected words in
favor of objects for their discourse. One could alternatively, and perhaps at less expense, follow Molloy's
suggestion and "obliterate texts . . . fill in the holes
of words till all is blank and flat and the whole ghastly
business looks like what it is, senseless, speechless, is-
sueless misery." [23]

There is doubtless a progression like this operating
in the central twenty years of Beckett's career, most
notably in the trilogy. It has been commonly assessed
as an inevitable process of formal decay—a view that
has received strong encouragement from Beckett's own
despairing comments. Yet Beckett is far from being as
helpless as he appears. It is important to stress that imitative form accounts not only for the "decay" of his art
over this period but also for its highest fruition: that
these works are not simply parts of a progression, but
also autonomous projects. They are a succession of raids
on the same enduring collection of mysteries, more or
less narrowly conceived. And the attack in each case
is an independent experiment with the imitative potential of certain formal elements of fiction: the archetypal
pattern, the narrator, the report, the two-part form,
storytelling, the tale of espionage, and the text itself.

13

Thus, in treating the works of this period, in particular *Watt, Molloy, Malone Dies,* and *The Unnamable,* I have focussed upon the key formal elements that in each case were the subjects of Beckett's most vigorous experimentation.

In the trilogy the idea of a progression appears to have come as an afterthought. I believe Beckett became more and more intrigued with the idea of pursuing the method of imitative form to the point where his subject would overwhelm his art. It is more than likely this notion led him to punctuate the trilogy by gathering up what appears to be the detritus of *The Unnamable* and publishing it together as *Texts pour rien* in 1955. Yet the progression, however contrived, led to an acute crisis. Once at the end of the process, Beckett found no way to reverse it. And, of course, logically there was no way to proceed—none, that is, unless he relinquished the method of imitative form altogether. And this, in fact, was what he did. In 1959, four years after the publication of *Texts pour rien,* Beckett spoke of the possibility of separating form from "chaos" in such a way that the order that is form does not carry over and pervert the chaos. "What I am saying does not mean that there will henceforth be no form in art. It only means that there will be new form, and that this form will be of such a type that it admits the chaos and does not try to say that the chaos is really something else. The form and the chaos remain separate. The latter is not reduced to the former." [24] When he said this he was already hard at work on precisely this task of separation. It was realized with the publication of *Comment c'est* in 1961.

This attempt to preserve the mysteries that are his literary occasion, first by bringing form into closer and closer expressive accord with them, then by releasing form from these mysteries entirely, provides a drama of its own in the course of Beckett's literary career. And the burden of my study is to show how this drama unfolds. Before Beckett even began exploring the possibilities of imitative form, however, he published two preliminary fictional experiments in the thirties. These are *More Pricks Than Kicks* (1934) and *Murphy* (1938). We shall, accordingly, begin with these. Perhaps more than anything else, they bear witness right at the start of his career to the remarkably diverse and improvisatory nature of Beckett's fiction.

1

Early Fiction

IN 1932 BECKETT published a short story entitled "Dante and the Lobster"; in the same year he worked on and abandoned a novel *Dream of Fair to Middling Women*. Both the short story and passages from the novel reappeared together, considerably revised, two years later. This was Beckett's first published book of fiction, *More Pricks Than Kicks*. But in the same year Beckett also published a peculiar short story entitled "A Case in a Thousand." [1] It is a rather neglected piece and has never to my knowledge been reprinted. Yet its brevity (two thousand words) and compactness allow us to see a lot more clearly than in *More Pricks* what Beckett was trying to do with fiction at this stage of his career.

The guise Beckett adopts for this story is that of the well-read incompetent. He has read hundreds of novels and short stories and is familiar with their fictional conventions. What escapes him is the fictional unity to which they usually belong and the coherent reality to which they are usually supposed to relate. For example, in handling plot he has grasped the strategy of developing a mystery through a series of tantalizing, and in this case sexual, innuendos. But the solution to the mystery is too "trivial and intimate" for him to burden us with. The plot has no closure, no proper ending, like a musical piece developed strongly in a particular key which fails to end on the tonic.

The subject of the story is the relationship of Dr.

Nye and Mrs. Bray. More precisely, it is the question of what exactly that relationship is. Dr. Nye works in the hospital in which Mrs. Bray's son is dying. Outside the hospital, Mrs. Bray keeps a daily vigil, watching her son's window. On the day of the story, Dr. Nye is told of her strange vigil but remains uninterested until he is informed that she has a family in Tuam.

"Then it is as I feared," he responds, "the woman is my old nurse."

From here, Beckett develops the mystery through a succession of broad hints. Dr. Nye goes out to meet her. Their talk turns to "the good old days": " 'Yes,' said Mrs. Bray, 'you were always in a great hurry to grow up so's you could marry me' "; but, Beckett adds, she "did not reveal the trauma at the root of this attachment." The days pass, and they begin seeing each other often in her son's room where Dr. Nye is in charge. Intently she watches the doctor's face "in the hope of recognizing him as the creature she had once cared." Dr. Nye is as keenly aware of her: "there was always something he wanted to ask her with reference to the good old days, but he felt it was neither the time nor the place, and this feeling grew steadily stronger." Once, in the course of his examination of Mrs. Bray's son, the doctor's face is overcome with an expression "at once aghast and rapt," and Mrs. Bray is moved "to gratification that at last she saw him as she could remember him; to shame, as the memory grew defined." Immediately after her son dies, they find themselves momentarily unable to part, yet unable to speak their minds. When at last they do part, Dr. Nye goes off to the seaside only to hurry back when he hears that Mrs. Bray is "back at her old games." The final encounter between them ends the story:

> On the bridge they met face to face. They moved into a recess in the parapet out of the noise, they leaned out over the water.
>
> "There's something I've been wanting to ask

most of the book's few readers have had serious reservations about its success. Yet the major cause of dissatisfaction—and an understandable one—has been a tendency to read it as an imitation of life rather than as what it is: an imitation of fictional conventions. If "life" can be called the subject of the book, it is only so generally by indirection—as a subject *in absentia*. The book seems to be fully enjoying the ultimate hoax that it is a novel. In the face of virtually no unity of plot or theme, it brazenly calls attention to the slightest links between chapters. One discovers footnotes such as "Cf. *Fingal*" (p. 151)[2] or comes across explicit cross-references in the text itself: "Belacqua had come unstuck like his own favour of Veronica in *What a Misfortune*" (p. 269); "What was left was just a fine strapping lump of a girl or woman, theatre nurse in *Yellow* from the neck down" (p. 274); "Alba Perdue, it may be remembered, was the nice little girl in *A Wet Night*" (p. 180).[3] Even the name of its hero—Belacqua Shuah—contains an imitation of the book's own literary flight and disaster. To reinforce this self-conscious literary quality, the book opens with Belacqua being torn as it were from the epic that gave him his name: "It was morning and Belacqua was stuck in the first of the canti in the moon. He was so bogged that he could move neither backward nor forward." He is reading the *Comedia* in preparation for his Italian lesson and is as "bogged" and out of place in that work as he is in Beckett's.[4]

The height of literary self-consciousness in *More Pricks Than Kicks* is the chapter entitled "A Wet Night." It deserves special attention for it is in this chapter that Beckett develops an actual substantive theme of expressive failure which gives point to his literary and stylistic posturing. In structure the story follows Belacqua and a few others as they prepare to go (or in Belacqua's case, delay going) to a party to be held by "the Frica." The preparations of the Alba are described in terms very similar to those Pope used for

you," he said, looking at the water where it flowed out of the shadow of the bridge.

She replied, also looking down at the water: "I wonder would that be the same thing I've been wanting to tell you ever since that time you stretched out on his bed."

There was a silence, she waiting for him to ask, he for her to tell.

"Can't you go on?" he said.

Thereupon she related a matter connected with his earliest years, so trivial and intimate that it need not be enlarged on here, but from the elucidation of which Dr. Nye, that sad man, expected great things.

"Thank you very much," he said, "that was what I was wondering."

They watched the water flowing out of the shadow a little longer, then she said she must be going. Dr. Nye took a box out of his pocket.

"I brought you a few peppermint creams," he said.

So they parted, Mrs. Bray to go and pack up her things and the dead boy's things, Dr. Nye to carry out Wasserman's test on an old schoolfellow.

Beckett's "achievement" here fits easily into the context of twentieth-century experimentation with plot. Like his peers, he is attacking the beginning-middle-end-mindedness which plotted works reinforce. Yet Beckett's method involves more than simply sabotaging plot, and it is in this that the uniqueness of both "A Case in a Thousand" and *More Pricks Than Kicks* lies. Beckett mounts his attack on closure on all fronts (conventions of situation, scenic description, authorial attitude, characterization, and so on) where other authors often attack it in plot alone, granting their characters and incidents life and coherence. Thus, the subject of "A Case in a Thousand"—Dr. Nye and Mrs. Bray and their relationship—is really of no importance whatsoever. What is important is the conventions in which it appears. One is tempted, perhaps, to describe such writing with such a worn label as "antifiction" in that it is so completely an attack on what the public would expect in, let us say, the "popular" fiction of 1934. What distinguishes this early work is the completeness of its negativity. It is work of pure destruction.

Observe, for example, the passage in which Dr. Nye reaches his decision to have the boy operated on. It begins on a particularly grave note. He feels he must tell Mrs. Bray of his decision. They wait in silence in the room together. Then suddenly our narrator ends the passage: "Mrs. Bray again closed her eyes as she felt the imposition too pregnant for words of his hand on the crown of her hat (which nothing could ever induce her to leave off), the rapid flutter of his fingers down her cheek, the ineffable chuck to her dewlap. She turned her face toward her son." Dr. Nye's gesture is admirably described. But it leaves a gaping hole in the incident as well as in his character—whatever that is.

Toward the beginning of the story, Dr. Nye has a mental experience. The convention Beckett is parodying is unmistakable: genus, sudden insight; species, profound illumination. "Without warning a proposition sprang up in his mind: Myself I cannot save." There is, granted, a weak comic closure between this and the "salvation" provided by Mrs. Bray. But there is no closure with the other passages characterizing Dr. Nye. The kind of fictional character capable of having profound inspirations in this mode, however comic, is hard to integrate with the kind of man described a few lines later: "The group on the bridge had crossed over to the other parapet, with the result, most pleasing to Dr. Nye, that where formerly he had seen their faces, now he enjoyed a clear view of their buttocks, male and female." And this incident, in turn, fails to "close" with anything else in the tale, just as, conversely, no single aspect of Dr. Nye is developed to the point where we can take him seriously as a character.

20

What was later to become one of Beckett's trad marks is the violent collision of conventions. The b example of this in "A Case in a Thousand" is the scription of Dr. Nye's reaction to the death of the b "Dr. Nye tried hard to recapture the sensation which a medical student he had experienced when a b died under his hand, just as he had it nicely spi for a lumbar puncture. He succeeded up to a p The blush gathered together like a wave in his ent sweeping aloft and breaking in his heart—this mu least he was permitted to re-enact." What adds peculiar impact of this passage is that the defla "nicely spitted for a lumbar puncture"—preced prose balloon—"the blush gathered like a wave If this is a reason for discomfort, however, it is if the story is read as parody or satire, which br to my final point: though Beckett's prize tool tainly parody, he is not writing parody in th tional sense. His end, in this story at least, is n credit any particular style but all styles. His st the coherence that any decent parody would the passage quoted above, neither line sur collision.

I don't think we can credit this story with " and enchantment of true experience." Still t intent is serious. "A Case in a Thousand," More Pricks Than Kicks, can be viewed a necessary demolition work. Many classica had to be brought down before Beckett work on his own Chartres. Of course, the inexperienced, too. To overlook this would him appear too fully in control of his des using what was available to him—convent easily master but which he chose to mishan

The greatest challenge of a book the Pricks Than Kicks was the scope it Beckett's talents for failure. Destructi carried out on a much vaster scale. An done while maintaining interest. Littl

Belinda and contrast nicely with the more Hudibrastic description of the Frica's toilette. Then the party begins, rages for almost thirty pages, and at last Belacqua and the Alba make their escape.

Belacqua is accosted by a Bovril sign even before making human contact in the story. Later he is troubled by an advertisement for a "brassier cum-corset décolleté." The Bovril sign dances "through its seven phases" ("The lemon of faith jaundiced, annunciating the series, was in a fungus of hopeless green reduced to shingles and abolished. Whereupon the light went out, homage to the slain. A sly ooze of gules . . ." [p. 61]), and the newspaper ad admonishes: "If the bust be too cogently controlled, then shall fat roll from scapula to scapula. If it be made passable and slight, then shall the diaphragm bulge and be unsightly" (p. 68). Between these two attacks by the media, Belacqua is barraged by "the homespun poet" and by Chas—"a highbrow bromide of French nationality with a diabolical compound of Skeat's and Paganini's and a mind like a tattered concordance" (pp. 64–65). Once Belacqua achieves relative safety from these dangers, we leave him to follow several parties in their progress toward the Frica's. A debate develops between "the Polar Bear" (who "never used the English word when the foreign pleased him better") and a Jesuit on the subject of music and belief. "The homespun poet" rehearses his poem "Calvary by Night":

rocket of bloom flare flower of night wilt for me
on the breasts of the water it has closed it has made
an act of floral presence on the water. [P. 75]

Chas, the "clockwork Bartlett," stops "to explain the world" to a group of students before catching his tram:

"The difference, if I may say so——"
"Oh," cried the students, *una voce*, "oh please!"
"The difference, then, I say, between Bergson

23

and Einstein, the essential difference, is as between philosopher and sociolog."

"Oh!" cried the students.

"Yes" said Chas, casting up what was the longest divulgation he could place before the tram, which had hove into view, would draw abreast.

"And if it is the smart thing now to speak of Bergson as a cod"—he edged away—"it is that we move from the Object"—he made a plunge for the tram—"and the Idea to Sense"—he cried from the step—"and Reason."

"Sense" echoed the students "and reason!"

The difficulty was to know exactly what he meant by *sense.*

"He must mean *senses*" said a first, "smell, don't you know, and so on."

"Nay said a second, "he must mean *common sense.*"

"I think" said a third, "he must mean *instinct,* intuition, don't you know, and that kind of thing."

A fourth longed to know what Object there was in Bergson, a fifth what a sociolog was, a sixth what either had to do with the world. [Pp. 77–78]

The full masquerade of sounds begins shortly after this at the Frica's. The Frica, by the way, has already been introduced to us in a very literary, indeed bookish, emblem: "Behold the Frica, she visits talent in the Service Flats. In she lands, singing Havelock Ellis in a deep voice, frankly itching to work that which is not seemly. Open upon her concave breast as on a lectern lies Portigliotti's *Penombre Claustrali,* bound in tawed caul. In her talons earnestly she grasps Sade's *Hundred Plays* and the *Anterotica* of Aliosha G. Brignole-Sale, unopened, bound in shagreened caul" (p. 66). The party guests are introduced by an epic catalogue: "Two banned novelists, a bibliomaniac and his mistress, a paleographer, a violist d'amore with his instrument in a bag, a popular parodist with his sister and six daughters, a still more popular Professor of Bullscrit and Comparative Ovoidology . . ." (p. 88). The poet recites his poem; Chas recites a piece of Old French; Mr. Larry O'Murcahaodha sings in Gaelic; the verbal whirlwind rises; the author moans:

> "The bicuspid" from the Ovoidologist "monotheistic fiction ripped by the Sophists, Christ and Plato, from the violated matrix of pure reason."
> Who shall silence them, at last? Who shall circumcise their lips from speaking, at last? [P. 108]

Belacqua and the Alba finally escape, with the Frica in hot pursuit. Belacqua eventually leaves the Alba in the small hours, discards his shoes, and at last sits on the curb in the rain and the silence. The climax of the chapter occurs here at the very end. Balacqua has a momentous experience—he discovers his hands: "What was that? He shook off his glasses and stooped his head to see. That was his hands. Now who would have thought of that! He began to try would they work, clenching them and unclenching, keeping them moving for the wonder of his weak eyes. Finally he opened them in unison, finger by finger together, till there they were, wide open, face upward, rancid, an inch from his squint . . ." (p. 112). The epiphany is an apt comment on the verbal unreality that precedes it.

What we have observed in this chapter is a conspiracy of noise—noise masquerading as communication. The chapter, indeed, comes close to being a satire of a gallery of grotesques. Yet the grotesques function not so much as representative types as they do vehicles for representative kinds of expression. This becomes clearer when the chapter is read in the context of the book as a whole, which offers neither consistent satiric butts nor a consistent sympathetic portrait of Belacqua and in which the posturing of these grotesques is of a piece with the posturing of the author.

One way in which stylistic disruption is achieved in

More Pricks Than Kicks is through the use of distinct stylistic departures for certain chapters as a whole. "A Wet Night" departs from the others in being more densely textured and more heavily larded with foreign and recondite terms. There are at least three other chapters that are also characterized by sustained stylistic deviations. The most noticeable is the impassioned love letter by the Smeraldina Rima which constitutes "The Smeraldina's Billet Doux": "Bel Bel my own beloved, *allways* and for *ever* mine!! Your letter is soked in tears death is the only thing. . . ." This extends for about ten pages. The first half of "Love and Lethe" is written in popular magazine fiction style, of the prize-winning variety, all the proper details of the domestic subject being scrupulously attended to by the narrator:

> The Toughs, consisting of Mr. and Mrs. and their one and only Ruby, lived in a small house in Irish Town. When dinner, which they took in the middle of the day, was ended, Mr. Tough went to his room to lie down and Mrs. Tough and Ruby to the kitchen for a cup of coffee and a chat. [P. 117]

> "Where are you going?" she said. She had the natural curiosity of a mother in what concerns her child.
> "Don't ask me" answered Ruby, who was inclined to resent all these questions. [P. 118]

> "Half-two!" ejaculated Mrs. Tough, who had no idea it was so late. [P. 118]

"Ding-Dong" is the only chapter with a first-person narrator. "I know all this," he writes, "because he (Belacqua) told me. We were Pylades and Orestes for a period . . . the relation abode and was highly confidential while it lasted" (p. 44). Later he confides: "I

gave him up in the end because he was not *serious*"
(p. 46). In addition to this first-person narrator and
his long commentaries on Belacqua's thought and behavior, the story is distinguished by a carefully contrived structure of suspense. As such, it is quite similar
to "A Case in a Thousand." "One day," the narrator
writes, "he gave me an account of one of these 'moving
pauses'"; and later, "But on this particular occasion . . ."; and then, "To this day he does not know
what caused him to look up, but look up he did." The
formula is obvious. What Belacqua looks up at from
his seat in the pub is a gross parody of fictional symbol-
ism: an old woman hawking "seats in heaven." "Her
speech was that of a woman of the people, but a gentle-
woman of the people. Her gown had served its time, but
yet contrived to be respectable. He noticed with a pang
that she sported about her neck the insidious little
mock fur so prevalent in tony slumland. . . . The features were null, only luminous, impassive and secure,
petrified in radiance . . ." (pp. 55–56). Embarrassed
beyond measure, Belacqua buys four "seats" and flees.
As in "A Case in a Thousand," the climax is a dud.

It is tempting to think that Beckett was perhaps inspired to compose in this way by Joyce's use of "technics" in *Ulysses*. There are certainly other strong parallels between the two authors and in particular between
"A Wet Night" and "The Dead," as Ruby Cohn has
noted;[5] and the book has its share of humorous allusions to the master. The Purefoy triplets appear at
Belacqua's wedding, and the ending of "The Dead" is
directly parodied at the end of "A Wet Night": "the
rain fell in a uniform untroubled manner. It fell upon
the bay, the littoral, the mountains and the plains, and
notably upon the central bog it fell with a rather
desolate uniformity" (pp. 112–113). At least one allusion to *Finnegans Wake* is forcibly wedged into the
narrative:

A divine creature, native of Leipzig, to whom Belacqua, roundabout the following Epiphany, had occasion to quote the rainfall for December as cooked in the Dublin University Fellows' Garden, ejaculated:
"Himmisacrakrüzidirkenjesusmariaundjosefundblütigeskreuz!"
Like that, all in one word. The things people come out with sometimes! [P. 112]

In addition, Beckett's mean style was I think noticeably affected by Joyce's not only in humor but in the close attention given to the rhythm and balance of sentence structure. Finally, like *Dubliners* and *Ulysses*, *More Pricks Than Kicks* could be called an anatomy of Dublin, and Belacqua is a kind of Ulysses with about the same scope of accomplishment as Joyce's protagonists.

Any extensive comparison, however, between Joyce's use of "technics" in *Ulysses* and Beckett's in *More Pricks* is doomed. For Joyce's aims were positive where Beckett's are negative. The clarity of Joyce's vision was a factor of the conventions employed; through them he achieved a multiplication of his powers. In *More Pricks Than Kicks* the effect is the reverse. The technics are introduced to war with the styles employed in other chapters, so that we ask ourselves, "Can these characters and incidents belong to the same world?" Even within the longer stylistic flights, Beckett is constantly bringing us back to earth with intrusions in another style. Where Joyce strove for the coherence of his episodes, Beckett is striving for their disruption. He is always anxious to let the gas out before it builds up too much pressure.

It is not surprising, then, that the mode of parody Beckett should develop most fully is that of the short flight. It appears everywhere in *More Pricks Than Kicks* and in great variety:

Hark, it is the season of festivity and goodwill. Shopping is in full swing, the streets are thronged with revelers, the corporation has offered a prize for the best-dressed window, Hyam's trousers are down again. [P. 61]

"And then . . . ?"
And then! Winnie take thought! [P. 26]

The sister of the parodist passed on to such as were curious what little she and her dear nieces knew of the Alba who was much spoken of in certain virtuous circles to which they had access, though to be sure how much of what they heard was true and how much mere idle gossip they were really not in a position to determine. However, for what it was worth, it appeared . . . [P. 92]

But *Tempux edax,* for now he is happily married to Lucy and the question of cicisbei does not arise. They sit up to all hours playing the gramophone. *An die Musik* is a great favourite with them both, he finds in her big eyes better worlds than this, they never allude to the old days when she had hopes of a place in the sun. [P. 158]

The voices of the author by this means become as various as the voices of his grotesques. And similarly they fail to become part of any coherent mockery of the world. What is mocked, in almost every case, is the mode of expression represented. Existing in such variety and with such complete separation from one another as well as the "story" that contains them, they suggest a variety of impossible worlds. Let us take another example, with its context, to clarify my point. Winnie and Belacqua, outside the walls of The Portrane Lunatic Asylum, are at odds whether to go over the wall or see the banks. They are in the presence of an automaton-like gardener whom the author has placed rather gratuitously outside the walls. Winnie solves the problem:

> "If we went on now" said Winnie "now that we have come so far, and followed the banks *down,* how would that be?"
> They agreed, Belacqua and the man, that it needed a woman to think these things out. Suddenly there was a tie between them.
> The tower began well . . . [P. 30]

The line in the sentimental mode—"suddenly there was a tie between them"—is a hole, punched as it were, right through the narrative. Through it we glimpse for a second a totally different world with all its different kinds of characters, states of mind, relationships, and situations. Because the reader knows nothing about the gardener and is almost as ignorant of Belacqua's character, the comic effect of the scene cannot be attributed to a mockery of either of the men. Rather it is derived from the sentence itself and the world it implies. It is the convention and its pretension to some kind of verisimilitude which are destroyed.

Actually there are two targets; the other being the reader who, as a reader of novels, finds it hard to get out of the habit (Habit) of trying to perceive some coherence in what he reads. These brief flights of parody—which are far worse than lacunae—keep recurring to plague him. Introduced without modulation from or to their contexts, they result in the same kind of frustration of closure which occurred in "A Case in a Thousand." We perceive people in this "novel," involved, doing things, coming together, going to parties, attempting suicide, dying, and being in love. Yet any feelings we may develop for them or opinions we may form about their significance are constantly being short-circuited by these intrusions.

Closely connected with this technique is Beckett's manipulation of his authorial image. Just as his text is a flux of shifting styles, his image is a flux of shifting attitudes. He is alternately bored and amused, indifferent and exasperated. At times he mocks his characters, and at times his readers. At times he appears totally capricious and at times grimly serious.

> Well, thought Belacqua, it's a quick death, God *help* us all.
> It is not. [P. 20]

Moreover, the text is riddled with interjections that reflect a complete indifference to the value or success of the book itself:

> Let us call it winter, that dusk may fall now and a moon arise. [P. 18]

> This may be premature. We have set it down too soon, perhaps. Still, let it bloody well stand. [P. 119]

> (this is very deep . . . [P. 123])

> The gas seems to be escaping somewhere. [P. 136]

> As material for anagogy (Greek g if you don't mind) . . . [P. 273]

One is tempted to locate behind such authorial disdain a controlling authorial personality. Yet, if one does, one is faced with the final difficulty of reconciling it with the fact that the author has, after all, taken the trouble to compose the book, to give it characters and chapters, and to publish it.

Caught in this flux of parodies and authorial attitudes is Belacqua. His "character" in turn is a patchwork of fictional types. He is the Victorian stoic, the

31

materialist, the man of sentiment, the cynic, the devoted lover, the buffoon, and the sympathetic isolato. Of course, other writers have combined any number of these traits in their antiheroes, but the difference is that they attempt, and often achieve, coherent combinations. Beckett's standards are the opposite. The flights of parody do not blend but collide. He is the paramour of Winnie (who was "pretty, hot and witty, in that order") and the devoted husband of the crippled Lucy; he is a pompous babbler in "Fingal" and a victim of pompous babble in "A Wet Night"; he is horrified by the death of a lobster and indifferent to the death of a child. "For we assume the irresponsibility of Belacqua," the author comments with shocking candor at one point, "his faculty for acting with insufficient motivation, to have been so far evinced in previous misadventures as to be no longer a matter for surprise" (p. 122). In "a swagger sports roadster chartered at untold gold by the hour" he drives so fast and recklessly that he smites "off the wheel of a growler as cleanly as Peter Malchus's ear after the agony" and scatters little children "like chaff." Then in a sudden panic before Victoria Bridge he stops the car, gets out, and pushes "her across with the help of a by-stander." He drives "quietly on through the dee-licious afternoon" to pick up his latest, Ruby Tough. For what?— their joint suicide, which turns out to be the other act of darkness. "L'Amour et la Mort—caesure—n'est qu'une mesme chose," the author quotes. For what it is worth.

This interpretation of *More Pricks Than Kicks*, like that of "A Case in a Thousand" is almost totally neglectful of the characters and action as things to be taken seriously in their own right. My argument has been that the true or serious subject of the book is its composition —the wide range of expressive forms that it attacks. It is only fair to note that there have been interpretations

that take the "content" of this book a lot more seriously
—I am thinking particularly of Raymond Federman's
interpretation in *Journey to Chaos*.[6] Federman and
others see more coherence in Belacqua and his story
than I am capable of seeing. This is our essential difference, and I have accordingly shifted the emphasis to
where I think it should belong.

It should also be noted that there are aspects of the
book which resist my interpretation. I mean in particular its tendency in odd passages to break what could be
called its pace of discontinuity. In such passages the
book would actually appear to be taking itself seriously as fiction. The following excerpt, for example,
undeniably comments on the world with Swiftian bit-
terness:

> All day the roadway was a tumult of buses, red and
> blue and silver. By one of these a little girl was
> run down, just as Belacqua drew near to the rail-
> way viaduct. She had been to the Hibernian
> Dairies for milk and bread and then she had
> plunged out into the roadway, she was in such a
> childish fever to get back in record time with her
> treasure to the tenement in Mark Street where she
> lived. The good milk was all over the road and the
> loaf, which had sustained no injury, was sitting
> up against the kerb, for all the world as though a
> pair of hands had taken it up and set it down
> there. The queue standing for the Palace Cinema
> was torn between conflicting desires: to keep
> their places and to see the excitement. They craned
> their necks and called out to know the worst, but
> they stood firm. Only one girl, debauched in ap-
> pearance and swathed in a black blanket, fell out
> near the sting of the queue and secured the loaf.
> With the loaf under her blanket she sidled un-
> challenged down Mark Street and turned into
> Mark Lane. When she got back to the queue her

place had been taken of course. But her sally had not cost her more than a couple of yards. [Pp. 49–50]

Neither can one ignore the fact that often Beckett is quite simply having a good time. There is a quantity of amusement in the book, which is provided for little more than the elementary task of entertaining either the reader or the author: "But nature takes care of her own and a loud rending noise was heard. Una stopped laughing and remained perfectly still. Her bodice had laid down its life to save hers" (p. 181). Occasionally, Beckett develops his humor secretively, lodging private jokes here and there for the attentive reader. Here is the way Alba Perdue asks to be taken home from the party in "A Wet Night":

> He was getting on nicely . . . when the Alba had a sudden idea and stopped him.
> "See me home" she said. [P. 110]

After a long absence from the pages the Alba reappears in the wedding party of "What a Misfortune" only to take her leave from the novel for good:

> She had a sudden idea.
> "See me home" she said to Walter. [P. 204]

Ninety-four pages separate the two passages. Fifty-one pages after the Alba's exit, Beckett calls the roll of Belacqua's past favorites: "Thelma née bboggs perished of sunset and honeymoon that time in Connemara. Then shortly after that they suddenly seemed to be all dead, Lucy of course long since, Ruby duly, Winnie to decency, Alba Perdue in the natural course of being seen home" (pp. 255–256). The little jokes are the reader's reward (or punishment) for reading so closely.

34

There is always the possibility, as Hugh Kenner suggests, that the twenty-eight-year-old author of *More Pricks Than Kicks* is still "not clear whether he is a comic writer or simply a bitter one." [7] Most critics who have read the book have had their reservations about his success. The chapters often do seem to be "written with a heavy and amateurish irony" as Frederick Hoffman complained,[8] and it has not been my intention to clear the book of all charges against it, or to revive it as a modern "classic." I have been primarily concerned to show that much of the bad writing is bad for a purpose: that the well-read incompetent was indeed a calculated guise. This is, quite simply, the best way to explain the sheer variety of failure which we have observed in *More Pricks*. The explanation has, moreover, the advantage of "placing" the book as a direct result of views that Beckett had already formulated in his essay on Proust. As we noted in the introduction, Beckett made a clear connection in that essay between the tyrants Habit and Memory and the conventional forms of the novel. In art, destroying the former is contingent upon destroying the latter, and it was the guise of the well-read incompetent which allowed Beckett to undertake a sweeping and systematic attack on fictional conventions in *More Pricks*.

This view of *More Pricks* not only has it looking back as it were to *Proust* but forward to the exhaustive use Beckett was to make of incompetence in his later work. Of course, his incompetence in *More Pricks* is by no means as "polished" as it is in the work of his maturity. It lacks the paradoxical combination of disorder and coherence which Beckett was to achieve in *Godot* and the trilogy. But most important, the book is limited in its serious purpose to an attack on fiction. The works of the forties, for all their strangeness, are much more authentically engaged in the ancient task of imitating life. This is due largely to the fact that

Beckett began in a sense as truly a well-read incompetent, better equipped to be a destroyer than a creator.

But there is also evidence, as we noted, that Beckett was actually uncertain as to precisely what kind of artist he wanted to be. Nothing shows this more clearly, I think, than *Murphy*, his second major work of fiction and, to my mind, his first and only novel.

2

Beckett's Novel

TRYING TO READ *More Pricks Than Kicks* is similar in ways to the experience Celia has in trying to read *Murphy*: "She felt . . . spattered with words that went dead as soon as they sounded; each word obliterated, before it had time to make sense, by the word that came next; so that in the end she did not know what had been said. It was like difficult music heard for the first time" (p. 40).[1] Yet, curiously, Murphy, of all Beckett's protagonists, is the least bewildering to the reader. His appearance at the beginning of the book is, granted, a shock. It is not often that one's protagonist is introduced strapped nude to a rocking chair by seven scarves. But in contrast to the first appearances of some of Beckett's other protagonists, Murphy's is more shocking than mysterious. We never do learn, for example, why Molloy is in his mother's bed, nor how he got there, nor why he writes, nor for whom. Yet long before Murphy's mind, body, and soul have been charted for us, we understand the reasons for his strange behavior. We understand him as well as we understand the other characters in the book. In short, though there is much that is shocking, there is little that is mysterious.

My argument in this chapter is that this understandability is tied to traditional aspects of novel form which Beckett employed in writing *Murphy* (1938). It is a widely recognized fact that traditional formal qualities are present in the book. It is "Beckett's sole exercise," as Kenner puts it, "and an anomalous one, in the work-manlike linkages of Flaubertian fiction." [2] Yet it is also widely felt that the traditional elements are important only insofar as they contribute to the "antifictional" character of the book. The following assessment comes closest perhaps to the consensus: "In spite of its dubious plot, *Murphy* remains a traditional novel. Undoubtedly the characters are intentionally presented as carica-tures, to fulfill the author's primary purpose of creating a work that mocks realism and rationalism. Therefore, the novel becomes a calculated intellectual exercise that coldly mirrors the world of man while subtly re-vealing the fraudulence of fiction." [3] My own view, however, is that in making major concessions to the form of the traditional novel—the destruction of which was the one serious purpose of *More Pricks Than Kicks* —Beckett made concessions as well to the thinking of the traditional novel. He appears to be of two minds: often yielding to the very form he tries to attack. Thus, there is more of tradition in *Murphy* than can be ac-counted for as fraud.

There is no denying, of course, that Beckett's "work-man like linkages" and elaborate subplot—"la course-poursuite d'Andromaque jouée par les Marx Brothers" [4] —are parody. The same is true of his scrupulous atten-tion to dates and places. Setting is provided as if on order:

> It burst on the floor without a sound, so that water is oozing towards the centre of the floor through-out the scene that follows. [P. 208]

> so that throughout the scene that follows Murphy's half of the bed is between her and them. [P. 231]

And details are often supplied with a polished irrele-vance: "In a somewhat similar way Celia had sat on Mr. Kelly's bed, and on Murphy's, though Mr. Kelly had had his shirt on" (p. 208). One finds in this novel, too, the same kind of disdain for the craft of fiction evidenced in *More Pricks*. Casually, Beckett punctures the suspension of disbelief: "The above passage is carefully calculated to deprave the cultivated reader" (p. 118).[5] Casually, he violates the contract with the reader: "Try it sometime, gentle skimmer" (p. 84). He intrudes to wrest the narrative from Ticklepenny or Celia or Cooper and give their accounts "expurgated, accelerated, improved, and reduced." The task of introducing the heroine is handed over to a table of vital statistics. And when his novel-machine finally begins to run down, he is there to chart its progress: "so all things hobble together for the only possible" (p. 227).

One finds, too, a continuation of Beckett's attack on the idiom and the conventional metaphor, inversions that in turn constitute a series of affronts to the novel shell in which they are contained:

The ceiling was lost in the shadows, yes, really lost in the shadows. [P. 64]

the Market, where the frenzied justification of life as an end to means threw light on Murphy's prediction. [P. 67]

strangled into a state of respiration. [P. 71]

Nothing can stop me now, was his last thought before he lapsed into consciousness. [P. 105]

The encounter, on which so much unhinges. . . [P. 114]

He broke into a sweat, lost all his yellow . . . [P. 164]

his own little dungeon in Spain. [P. 180]

The same holds true perhaps for Beckett's outrageous puns ("It was true that Cooper never sat, his acathisia was deep-seated and of long standing" [p. 119]). They remind us that the work, after all, is only a fabric of words, and that compared to the story the words, at least, are interesting.[6]

One even finds in *Murphy* the attempt to play with tonal shifts—the short flights of parody that Beckett used so extensively in *More Pricks*. Here are two examples, one providing gothic horror and one a sort of authorial bravado:

> The fall on the landing had cracked the mirror set in the flap. She stifled a cry, averted her head and handed him a large black envelope with the title in letters of various colours. [P. 30]

> Let us now take Time that old fornicator, bald though he may be behind, by such few sad short hairs as he has, back to Monday, October the 7th, the first day of his restitution to the bewitching Miss Greenwich. [P. 114]

But these flights are occasional. They are not only less frequent than in *More Pricks* but also represent a much fainter departure from the mean style. Conversely, it is easier to identify a mean style in *Murphy*. There is definitely a single mind behind the prose: an incorrigibly witty mind that loves to play with words and mock its subject, yet at the same time is more deeply involved in its task than the mind that produced *More Pricks*. Thus, even the wit will occasionally take on a certain earnestness, developing at times into a sarcastic belligerency that seems to lay the author bare: "This phrase is chosen with care, lest the filthy censors should lack an occasion to commit their filthy synecdoche" (p. 76). But a frequent effect of Beckett's wit is neither sympathy nor amusement, but exasperation.

The reason for this lies in the fact that Murphy and Celia become sympathetic characters and, in addition, there is a pronounced mellowing of tone throughout later parts of the book. It is as if the novel began to take itself seriously; by the last chapter there are some rather remarkable passages of description which are permitted to unroll totally unscathed:

> Late afternooon, Saturday, October the 26th. A mild, clear, sunless day, sudden gentle eddies of rotting leaves, branches still against the still sky, from a chimney a pine of smoke. [P. 276]

> The ludicrous fever of toys struggling skyward, the sky itself more and more remote, the wind tearing the awning of cloud to tatters, pale limit-less blue and green recessions laced with strands of scud, the light failing. . . . She watched the tandem coming shakily down from the turmoil, the child running forward to break its fall, his trouble when he failed, his absorbed kneeling over the damage. He did not sing as he departed, nor did she hail him. [P. 281]

A standpoint of sympathy, warmth and, by implication, value is established. It is allowed to develop too strongly to be cancelled by the intrusion of mockery. Therefore when mockery does intrude we feel an ex-asperation very different from the calculated exasper-ation of More Pricks Than Kicks. In short, Murphy, like a novel, has point of view, and the techniques Beckett developed in More Pricks to annihilate point of view do not properly belong to it.

Celia illustrates my argument best. She is, to begin with, superior to the other characters in her ability to understand and become like Murphy: "Thus in spite of herself she began to understand as soon as he gave up trying to explain. She could not go where livings were being made without feeling that they were being made away. She could not sit for long in the chair without the impulse stirring, tremulously, as for an exquisite depravity, to be naked and bound" (p. 67). And once Murphy abandons her, she actually develops the capacity to "come out in her mind," proceeding like her lover from one zone to the next:

> She closed her eyes and was in her mind with Murphy, Mr. Kelly, clients, her parents, others, herself a girl, a child, an infant. In the cell of her mind, teasing the oakum of her history. Then it was finished, the days and places and things and people were untwisted and scattered. She was lying down, she had no history. [Pp. 148–149]

It is worth noting that this experience occurs in the room formerly occupied by "the old boy." The latter, a foreshadowing of Beckett's future protagonists, appears as a projection of Celia's plight: "The old boy was believed to be a retired butler. He never left his room, except of course when absolutely obliged to, nor allowed anyone to enter it. He took in the tray that Miss Carridge left twice daily at his door, and put it out when he had eaten" (p. 69).[7] Celia, alone in her room that lies directly below the old boy's, becomes increasingly absorbed in the sound of his continual pacing overhead. After the old boy cuts his throat, the silence below is unbearable. She feels an "immense longing" to move into his room, which at last she does, bringing Murphy's rocker with her.

Throughout chapter eight the character of Celia is deepened. Her isolation is made poignant by a carefully structured series of abandonments. The account of the old boy's death is followed by Murphy's departure. He assures her that he will return—if he were leaving for good, he says, he would take his rocker. But she senses he is leaving for good and goes to the window to watch him depart: "As he passed the door, going towards Pentonville, she called down goodbye. He did not hear her, he was hissing" (p. 143). When after several days Murphy does not return, she goes to the Round Pond to seek her aged grandfather, Mr. Kelly. She waits throughout the afternoon in the rain, but Mr. Kelly fails to appear. The last person to leave the Gardens is a child. She watches him reel in his kite, dismantle it, and wrap it up. "As he passed the shelter Celia called good night. He did not hear her, he was singing" (p. 153).

Finally she also leaves the park: "She was tired and wet, Mr. Kelly had failed, the child had ignored her good night. There was nothing to go back to . . ." (p. 153). And when she does get back, she learns that Murphy has come and gone, taking his rocker with him. The final picture of Celia is remarkable and shows how well Beckett could define mood through the clean, precise depiction of gesture:

> When it was quite clear that this was the whole extent of the message Celia went on slowly up the stairs. Miss Carridge stood with a finger on the switch, watching. The turn of the stair took the body out of sight, but Miss Carridge could still see the hand on the banister, gripping, then sliding a little, gripping again, then sliding a little more. When the hand also disappeared Miss Carridge switched off the light and stood in the dark that was so much less extravagant, not to mention richer in acoustic properties, listening.
>
> She heard with surprise the door of the big room opened and closed again immediately. After a pause the steps resumed their climb, no more slowly than before, but perhaps a little less surely. She waited till she heard the old boy's door close,

neither loudly nor softly, and then went back to her book: *The Candle of Vision,* by George Russell (A. E.). [Pp. 154–155]

Remarkable in a different way is the ending of chapter ten. Throughout this chapter, Celia suffers the verbal barrage of Wylie, Neary, and Miss Counihan, an inane trio who have been pursuing Murphy throughout the novel. Their presence has increased the sense of Celia's isolation. Then, without any warning, flashbacks of Celia's infancy with Mr. Kelly alternate with babbling from the others. The montage provides—again with simplicity—a dimension of both Celia and Mr. Kelly which cannot be found anywhere else in the book:

> "I cannot believe he has left you," said Wylie.
> "He will come back," said Neary.
> "We shall be here to receive him," said Miss Counihan.
> Her cot had a high rail all the way around. Mr. Willoughby Kelly came, smelling strongly of drink, knelt, grasped the bars and looked at her through them. Then she envied him, and he her. Sometimes he sang.
> "Neary and I upstairs," said Wylie.
> "I here with you," said Miss Counihan.
> "Call the woman," said Neary.
> Sometimes he sang:
> *Weep not, my wanton, smile upon my knee,*
> *When thou art old, there's grief enough for thee,*
> etc. Other times:
> > *Love is a prick, love is a sting,*
> > *Love is a pretty pretty thing,*
> etc. Other times, other songs. But most times he did not sing at all. [P. 235]

44

Passages like these as well as the controlled sadness of the last chapter indicate beyond doubt that, if Beckett had wished, he could have achieved great success in a mode far different from the one he chose. By the very potential they reveal, such passages indicate how serious Beckett was when he chose to reject the traditional novel: that his later work was not just a matter of suiting his talents, but a deliberate choice of "failure" for serious artistic reasons.

But in *Murphy*, the competent sympathetic portraiture is marred by what William York Tindall called "a style often at odds with the matter." [8] For example, having established our sympathy for Celia in chapter eight, Beckett leaves her until the middle of chapter ten, when Wylie, Neary, and Miss Counihan arrive at Miss Carridge's. The first half of chapter ten is a sometimes marvelous parody of the novel of manners which seems to have generated a momentum that Beckett could not control. Thus when Celia is reintroduced she is caught by the mean style, as if infected by the trio of lovers who await her in the room below:

> "Bosom friends of Mr. Murphy," said Miss Carridge, "they came in a taxi."
> Celia raised her face. This caused Miss Carridge to add, in some confusion.
> "But I needn't tell you that. Forgive me."
> "Ah, yes, you need," said Celia, "omit no material circumstance, I implore you. I have been so busy, so busy, so absorbed, my swan crossword, you know, Miss Carridge, seeking the rime, the panting syllable to rime with breath, that I have been dead to the voices of the street, dead and damned, Miss Carridge, the myriad voices." [P. 229]

Perhaps, as Tindall suggests, this is to keep "what is moving at a distance—lest it be too moving." [9] If this was its intended function, it has nonetheless failed to prevent most readers, or at least most critics, from being moved by Celia. Beckett's acid wit, in other words, is not a consistent and effective technique employed to frustrate closure (as it was in *More Pricks Than Kicks*) but rather an intrusion (funny as it is) in what is basically a very moving portrait.

A more important point, however, is that both the tone of mockery, when confined to the lesser characters, and the moving portrait of Celia are products of the same orientation to the craft of fiction—a spirit and orientation fundamentally different from that of *More Pricks Than Kicks*. This brings us back to the understandability of Murphy. The tone and characterization of the novel imply that definite things can be said about life, that conclusions can be drawn, people understood, and evaluations made. And the coherent novel form serves to support this far more than the antifictional aspects of the work serve to attack it. Despite its mockery of conventions, the final effect of the novel is to admit the possibility of constructing an ordered mimetic form that will serve as a valid comment on experience. This is in sharp contrast to *More Pricks* and the later work.

Furthermore, though Beckett seems to be making use of the very novel structure he so elaborately builds up to attack what it represents, the mockery in the book is far more often directed *at the world* (a definite, inhabited world, which is the "occasion" for the mockery) than at the conventions in which the representatives of the world are found. It is a satirical novel. Satire and parody are directed outward—not inward in a process of mutual annihilation. And satire turned in the outward direction has the reverse effect of the inward variety. It asserts the validity of the form in which it is found—without which validity its effect would be nil.

For example, it is obviously not the convention in

46

which Miss Carridge is found which is being mocked but the spirit of hypocrisy and materialism she represents. She is part of a larger, angrier, and more direct social criticism that pervades the novel. Beckett is often shockingly (shockingly for Beckett) explicit. Murphy's purchase of 1.83 cups of tea for the price of one is a very direct comment on a materialistic society: "Only compare the belligerents. On the one hand a colossal league of plutomaniac caterers, highly endowed with the ruthless cunning of the sane, having at their disposal all the most deadly weapons of the postwar recovery; on the other, a seedy solipsist and fourpence" (p. 82). This becomes even more direct in Beckett's scathing denunciation of the sane attitude toward the insane. The family in charge of the Magdalen Mental Mercyseat, the Clinch clan, represents the constant and cruel threat a sane society poses for any who would prefer the pleasures of mind to the physical world. When Murphy, to Bom Clinch's great disgust, wishes to begin his work in the asylum right away, Beckett writes with an anger that is unmistakable, reaching out to include the *hypocrite lecteur:*

> Bom gave up. When the fool supports the knave the good man may fold his hands. The fool in league with the knave against himself is a combination that none may withstand. Oh, monster of humanity and enlightenment, despairing of a world in which the only natural allies are the fools and knaves, a mankind sterile with self-complicity, admire Bom feeling dimly for once what you feel acutely so often, Pilate's hands rustling in his mind. [P. 170]

"The issue . . . , as lovingly simplified and perverted by Murphy, lay between nothing less fundamental than the big world and the little world . . ." (p. 178). Perhaps Murphy has simplified and perverted

47

it, yet in its way the novel as a whole bears out this view of the issue with much the same simplicity. As Miss Counihan so movingly puts it, "There is a mind and there is a body" (p. 218). The characters in the novel are condemned, or awarded sympathy, first according to how fully they comprehend this, and second according to their abilities to appreciate the pleasures of the little world. On the one hand, Wylie, Neary, Miss Counihan, members of the sane world, being blind and driven by a clockwork biology, are accordingly condemned. Murphy, on the other hand, is a hero. And as such he is precisely the reverse of the later protagonists of Beckett's fiction and closer to the mainstream of fiction. He is gifted, not with incompetence, but comprehension.

The book, then, operates by a series of contrasts rather than collisions. One set of consistently developed characters is set against another, one way of behaving against another, one world against another. Mr. Endon ($\epsilon\nu\delta o\nu$ = within), the gentle schizophrenic at the Mercyseat, is established as an ideal. When what he represents is found to be impossible, the book provides the emphatic and bitter judgment: the Gardens are closed for the night, Murphy is asphyxiated, and his cremated remains are strewn on a barroom floor. Except for the drift in Beckett's mockery, which I noted earlier, there is a very solid sense of closure almost everywhere in the novel—characterization, point of view, mood, plot—a closure that is in the best of that tradition Beckett deplored in the essay on Proust.

Considerable critical discussion has been devoted to the intellectual content of *Murphy*, and again the stress has been on how the book fits *in* with the rest of the canon. Since the author devotes a whole chapter to "a justification of the expression 'Murphy's mind'" (p. 107), it is not surprising that a lot of attention has been given to the three "zones" of Murphy's mind defined therein, and more than once a parallel has been drawn between the succeeding stages that these zones represent and the succeeding stages of Beckett's literary canon.[10] Again I find myself in basic disagreement and my disagreement relates to the different mimetic character of the book which I have described so far. This is not to overlook the fact that the book, like all Beckett's work, is concerned with an intolerable situation. But first, and as I have argued so far, the reality that contains this intolerable situation in *Murphy* is ordered and comprehensible; and second, what I wish to show now, the nature of the intolerable situation in *Murphy* is quite different from that in the later work. It is, in short, a disharmony rather than a mystery. The distinction between these two words is admittedly my own, distorting the words, but it works for this analysis: disharmony pertains to pleasure and mystery to reality. To state it another way, the difference is one between hedonics and epistemology: the primary motive in *Murphy* is to escape, to ease the pressure; in the rest of the canon that motive remains, but it is bound up with a profounder motive to reveal, to be true, or at least to show how true we can be.

We can illustrate this difference with the figure of a man on a rack. On the one hand, we can accept the rack as a given order and concentrate solely on the man's attempts to harmonize the demands of his various limbs. If he attempts to ease the strain on one limb, the strain on the other limbs grows proportionately. And so on. What we are concerned with is the intolerable disharmony contained in a given order. On the other hand, we can shift our attention to the rack itself. Who controls it? What is the value of the pain? And so on. What we are concerned with now is a disharmony that is part of a larger mystery.

When we first see Murphy, strapped naked to his rocker, Beckett wastes no time in explaining that "he sat in his chair in this way because it gave him pleasure!" (p. 2). The exclamation point is provided not only as a rebuff to certain moral critics but also as an announcement of the subject: pleasure! In *Murphy* the central impossibility is pleasure. That life itself is impossible is not Beckett's immediate concern, and the Cartesian and occasionalist elements that abound in the novel are used primarily to construct a framework within which Murphy is contained.[11] Murphy, of course, is at a loss to comprehend where mind and body meet. But Beckett is not going to devote much time to portraying the agony of trying to comprehend this. "The problem was of little interest" (p. 109), he says. *Knowing* is not really important. What is important is enjoying. The book, therefore, can start with a number of postulates that constitute an order, the first of which is that there is a big world and a little world. The respective claims and pleasures of these worlds are different and of known value. What is important is making a pleasurable go of an existence in which such an order obtains.[12]

The basic order consists of two sets of coordinates: mind and body, self and other. What the book concludes is that, though they represent irreconcilable claims, there is no escaping any one of them. Just as we are constantly reminded that the claims of the body inevitably disrupt the pleasure of Murphy's mind, so the claims of the other inevitably disrupt the pleasure of isolation. The nature of life is in dependency. This last fact is movingly portrayed by Celia, mocked in the comic triangle and bitterly recognized in Murphy. Murphy even becomes dependent on the inmates of the Magdalen Mental Mercyseat for a surrogate experience of the little world.

In being concerned with harmonizing these four co-ordinates, it would follow that the novel would be concerned with love, which indeed it is. Love in its highest form, one could postulate, is a harmony of all four; mind, body, self, and other. Needless to say it is conspicuous by its absence. In its place we have lower

...deas of order to achieve the refined and ...iss of his master. In chapter five, Murphy ...e 120 ways in which his five biscuits may ...hen four of them are subsequently eaten ...w's dachshund, the soggy remainder be- ...ot commentary on the value of Murphy's ...s. Though the incident parallels Molloy's ...ts with his sucking stones, the character in ...orks who is closest to Murphy is Moran. ...en we first meet him, epitomizes the kind of ...ctured perception and behavior that Beck- ... in *Proust*. And yet Murphy comes very close ...n his fanatical adherence to the astrological ...ns of Pandit Suk. For that matter, an equally ...el would be Neary in his devotion to Herrn ...nd though Murphy finally abandons his ... at the M.M.M., the solipsism with which he ...it is described as system: "The more his own ...losed round him, the less he could tolerate its ...bordinated to any other. Between him and his ... doubt there was correspondence, but not in ...nse. They were *his* stars, he was the prior ... (pp. 182–183). This may be putting too much ...on Beckett's use of the term "system" in this ...; nevertheless there is considerable evidence ...Iurphy is not merely trapped in the order of ...orld but unable to dissociate his mind from order. ...is that excludes him from Mr. Endon's bliss.

...s view of the substantive content of *Murphy* does ...certain extent bring the book within the orbit of ...y developed in *Proust*. But I would like to end by ...hasizing the digressive nature of the work. The ...r substantive difference is this: the disorder in ...Endon's mind is not at all the disorder Beckett is ...erned with in *Proust*. The enchantment Beckett ...ks of in *Proust* is derived from a vision of the dis- ...er that is life—man, rack, and master; mind and ...y; self and other—in short, the "mess." The enchant-

forms of love which constitute the various stopgap solutions. There are primarily two, both realized by Murphy for brief passages of time and both involving a necessary fragmentation of the coordinates of the world. The first is his physical love with Celia, which harmonizes body and other. The word, by the way, with which he chooses to forestall the censors is more than a euphemism. For the term "music" makes it clear that pleasure, love, and harmony are inseparable concepts. With Celia, for the nights at least, he enjoys "serenade, nocturne, albada."

The other form of love is "the intellectual love in which alone he could love himself, because there alone he was lovable" (p. 179). It is the polar opposite of the first form, harmonizing as it does the mind and the self. We learn that "Murphy, while still less than a child, had set out to capture himself, not with anger but with love" (p. 201). This love is the "pleasure!" that Murphy experiences in his rocker. It is also a form of "music." When Murphy retreats in the interests of this pleasure to the Magdalen Mental Mercyseat, we are informed that "M.M.M. stood suddenly for music, MUSIC, MUSIC, in brilliant, brevier and canon, or some such typographical scream, if the gentle composer would be so friendly" (p. 236). We are left in no doubt as to which form of music is preferable. Mr. Endon represents a perfect harmony of self-sufficiency, while the bacchic melodies of Ticklepenny and Bom Clinch provide a ready index of the inferiority of physical love throughout the episodes at the Magdalen Mental Mercyseat.[13]

There is finally what one could call "anti-love." This is figured in the hapless Neary and arises from his figure-and-ground-mindedness. What Neary calls love or love's fulfillment is essentially a short circuit—"the glare of pursuit and flight extinguished" (p. 29). And though he earnestly desires this, he can never have it. Indeed, it is something he cannot tolerate for it is his nature to be constantly in motion as it were. In effect, anti-love is an aggravation of the worst kind of disharmony: constantly theorizing about a constant bodily need; constantly isolated and constantly in need of union.

The forms of harmony and disharmony can be rather nicely put in a simple paradigm. I think it is worth including here, if only to support further my contention that *Murphy* is one Beckett work that will oblige a demand for paradigms: [14]

LOVE
Perfect Harmony
of Mind, Body, Self, & Other

Music
Physical Harmony
with Other

Music, MUSIC, MUSIC
Mental Harmony
with Self

ANTI-LOVE
Neary's Figure & Ground
Extreme Disharmony
of Mind, Body, Self, & Other

We cannot leave it quite so neatly as that. The paradigm can stay, but there is one aspect of the music, MUSIC, and, most importantly, MUSIC, which must be dealt with. For MUSIC—the third zone of Murphy's mind—is at once the purest form of mental harmony and the purest form of disorder. Here is how it is described in chapter six:

a flux of forms, a perpetual coming together and falling asunder of forms . . . neither elements nor

states, noth
with the fr
love or hate
Here there
pure forms o
but a mote in
did not move,
conditioned ge
[P. 112]

The description of th
probably a very apt
stant mental state. Th
association of perfect
Neary, Wylie, and Miss
out often, are very prop
is a predictable, machine
flight. The chess game
Endon, on the other hand
way toward harmony—fo
Murphy's mind: keeping a
ble movements of the chess
ability and reason. The E
balances strategically with
Wylie, Neary, and Miss Cou
event that proceeds with cc
ordered game:

"You to play, Needle."
"And do the lady out o
Wylie. "And put the lady to
another! Reary, Neally!"
"No trouble," said Miss Cou
Now it was anybody's turn.

One could go further and ar
crowning flaw, in addition to his in
weakness for system. Though he is
asystematic chess with Mr. Endon

sullied with
permanent bl
computes the
be eaten. W
by Miss De
comes an a
computation
achievemen
the later
Moran, wh
rigidly str
ett derided
to Moran
admonitio
valid mo
Koffka.
astrology
replaces
system c
being su
stars no
Suk's s
system"
weight
contex
that M
this w
It is th
Thi
to a
theor
emph
majo
Mr.
con
spea
ord
bo

ment that Beckett is concerned with in *Murphy* is derived from escape, withdrawal from an ordered world to a disorder in the mind. The experience in *Proust* is a seeing of things as they are; the experience in *Murphy* is an escape from things as they are. The enchantment in *Proust* is mixed with agony; the enchantment in *Murphy* is unadulterated bliss.

The book is a curious anomaly, both in form and "doctrine." And the rest of the canon is a standing refutation of both its novel form and substantive content. Perhaps in its creation Beckett allowed himself a few myths. Certainly one was what he described as "Murphy's mind." For Murphy's third zone is a mythical pleasure zone of chaos, and there is nothing quite so pure or so soothing as chaos in the works that follow. Furthermore, "what [Murphy] called his mind functioned not as an instrument but as a place" (p. 178). That this is an impossibility is borne out by the constant flux and placelessness of what the speaker of *The Unnamable* called his mind. Mr. Endon is a phantom of delight. In the later works the only disorder of which the mind is capable is the experience of being— as agonizing as it is enchanting.

We have now come to the end of the first stage of our study as well as the first stage of Beckett's work in fiction. His two major works of the thirties show clearly that Beckett was of two minds about his craft. Thus after tearing down the house of fiction in 1934, he put it back up again in 1938. What followed next represents still another radical departure. Between 1938 and 1944 much transpired—the war, Beckett's work in the Underground, farm labor in the Vaucluse, a reading perhaps of Kafka's *Castle*—which contributed heavily no doubt to *Watt*. But of the two earlier works, it is the first with its extensive, though essentially destructive, use of incompetence which augurs the creative incompetence of Beckett's experiments with imitative form.

3

Imitative Form: The First Experiment

WATT REPRESENTS a change not only in formal strategy, but also in subject. It is, in Hoffman's phrase, an "epistemological farce." The subject has its fitting exemplum in Arsene's tale of Mr. Ash:

> One evening I ran into him on Westminster Bridge. It was blowing heavily. It was also snowing heavily. I nodded, heavily. In vain. Securing me with one hand, he removed from the other with his mouth two pairs of leather gauntlets, unwound his heavy woolen muffler, unbuttoned successively and flung aside his great coat, jerkin, coat, two waistcoats, shirt, outer and inner vests, coaxed from a wash-leather fob hanging in company with a crucifix I imagine from his neck a gunmetal half-hunter, sprang open its case, held it to his eyes (night was falling), recovered in a series of converse operations his original form, said, Seventeen minutes past five exactly, as God is my witness, remember me to your wife (I never had one), let go my arm, raised his hat and hastened away. A moment later Big Ben (is that the name?) struck six. This in my opinion is the type of all information whatsoever, be it voluntary or solicited. [Pp. 45–46] [1]

56

On the face of it, "the type of all information" Arsene is teaching is revealed in the discrepancy between 5:17 and 6:00. "If you want a stone, ask a turnover" (p. 46). But the anecdote does much more. Uncertainty of information is Arsene's point, but the mystery of appearances is the true subject of the passage. What drives Mr. Ash? Why this great effort in bitter cold for the time? Why to Arsene? The entire exemplum sets up a whole set of relations which defies explanation. The best touch of all is Mr. Ash's death "of premature exhaustion, the following week." The paradigm, or perhaps antiparadigm, for the mystery of appearances is provided in the progression of Mr. Knott's servants:

Name	Physical Type
Vincent	Big bony, etc.
Walter	Big bony, etc.
Arsene	Little fat, etc.
Erskine	Little fat, etc.
Watt	Big bony, etc.
Arthur	Little fat, etc.
Micks	Big, powerful, placid, lymphatic

We have here the sense of order, yet we also have Arthur, and worse, Micks. We have the sense of significance, yet we have absolutely no way of telling what that significance is. This is the type of all appearances whatsoever. Watt's pathetic and doomed attempts to ascribe meanings to these appearances are what the book is about.

This marks a big change from *Murphy*. Concern has shifted from pleasure! to knowing, which is not to say, of course, that Watt is not searching, like Murphy, for relief, but simply that relief is now contingent on inducing some kind of meaning from events. As David H. Hesla writes in his essay on *Watt*, "Beckett's earlier hero, Murphy, sought not to achieve a pact of co-existence with reality, with the 'big world,' but was full of purpose to abdicate entirely from the colossal fiasco. Watt, on the other hand, is prepared to endure the big blooming buzzing confusion, but only on terms which will permit him to domesticate reality, to lead it about on a leash of words, to keep himself unspotted by the splash of things." [2]

It may, incidently, be argued that this is not properly an epistemological quest since Watt is not really concerned with knowing but simply with expressing, regardless of whether what he expresses comes anywhere near the meaning of its occasion. But this formulation of the problem is somewhat misleading. For Watt's failure stems directly from his growing concern, in spite of himself, for the real inexpressible meaning of things whether such real meaning really exists or not. He is a naïve Oedipus, as Ludovic Janvier calls him, an Oedipus gradually enlightened as to his naïveté by the Sphinx.[3] It is this that brings on his despair of language. The dilemma was first, I think, defined by Jacqueline Hoefer:

> In Watt's scientific and positivistic thought, to distinguish between what can be said about an event and what the event *really* means is sheer nonsense. Yet Watt persistently makes this distinction: he is content with an "outer meaning," which he can observe and make formulations about. But there is another kind of meaning, non-sensory and non-rational, indefinable in his terms, of which he is aware, though he purports to ignore its significance. Watt's awareness of this latter kind of meaning is the tragic flaw, so to speak, in his armor of logic and language.[4]

58

In this regard the situation in *Watt* is essentially the same as that in the trilogy. For all the resigned cynicism of the later heroes, they are plagued by the same sense of significance, the same failure of language, and the same obligation to express.

But the difference between *Watt* and *Murphy* is sharp. In fact, there is much to suggest that *Watt* is a kind of reply or rebuttal to *Murphy*. Thus the sexual harmonies of Murphy and Celia are answered by the muscial chairs of Watt and the fishwoman, Mrs. Gorman. And for that matter, all the attainable forms of music in *Murphy* are answered by the computerized krak, krek, krik of frogs which Murphy hears in a ditch. The voices in Watt's mind bring only bewilderment, as they sing unmelodic summaries of life which fail to resolve but leap at the finish to incredible A-sharps.[5] Watt's asylum is the M.M.M. revisited. The serene inmates of the M.M.M. are replaced by "scum, cluttering up the passageways, the hallways, grossly loud, blatantly morose, and playing at ball, always playing at ball, . . . this jocose this sniggering muck" (p. 153). Murphy's harmonies, the perfect and soothing disorders of mind, are not admitted, even in hypothesis. They are replaced by Sam's "that is perhaps something, perhaps something," a phrase that defines both the change in focus and awareness, and the source of frustration and pleasure. Mr. Knott, the answer to Mr. Endon, is fascinating not because of his hypothetical insides, but because of his bewildering outsides. The effort is no longer to *be* him but to comprehend him. Confusion is no longer a sublime district of the mind but an awesome process made manifest by Mr. Knott. What harmonies may exist in his mind are irrelevant. Our problem is the music he gives voice to:

From time to time, for no apparent reason, Mr. Knott opened his mouth in song. From bass to tenor, all male registers were employed by him, with equal success. He did not sing well, in Watt's opinion, but Watt had heard worse singers. The music of these songs was of an extreme monotony. For the voice, save for an occasional raucous sally, both up and down, to the extent of a tenth, or even an eleventh, did not leave the pitch at which, having elected to begin, it seemed obliged to remain, and finally to end. The words of these songs were either without meaning, or derived from an idiom with which Watt, a very fair linguist, had no acquaintance. [P. 208]

To define the change in formal strategy which coincided with the change in subject let us look at one of the many problems Watt has on the ground floor of Mr. Knott's house, I mean particularly the naming of the pot—the now famous pot that Watt used to serve Mr. Knott slops. The narrator, in his infinite patience, grants five pages to the subtleties of this problem, of which the following is a good sample:

Not that the fact of Erskine's naming the pot, or of his saying to Watt, My dear fellow, or, My good man, or, God damn you, would have changed the pot into a pot, or Watt into a man, for Watt, for it would not. But it would have shown that at least for Erskine the pot was a pot, and Watt a man. Not that the fact of the pot's being a pot, or Watt's being a man, for Erskine, would have caused the pot to be a pot, or Watt to be a man, for Watt, for it would not. [Pp. 83–84]

During these five pages, the narrator defines the problem. We understand Watt has difficulty fixing the pot with the word "pot." We understand he has the same problem fixing himself with the word "man." We understand this is painful for him; that there are certain possibilities of temporary relief; but there is nothing that will wholly reestablish the sufficiency of the erstwhile sufficient words "pot" and "man" for this thing and this Watt. Yet at the same time the narrator is explaining all this, the reader also *experiences* the insufficiency of words because of the form in which the explanation is put. Through the power of rhyme the narrator pounds the sense out of the words "pot" and "Watt," reducing them to "not." I am not claiming the reader's experience is precisely that of Watt, nor that through it he comprehends the ineffability of all things and experience. But the point is that the form is used to generate in the reader an experience approaching the experience that is its "content." In other words, Beckett is employing imitative form.

It is an argument of this kind which constitutes the climax of Hesla's essay. Hesla argues that in each section of *Watt* Beckett takes us on a circular journey around the periphery of its subject. In other words, we know the subject as an absence in much the same way Watt knows Mr. Knott. "Beckett has, as it were, located, defined Knott by reporting everything about him which is irrelevant, adiaphorous, and inconsequential: He has defined the Center of the novel, Mr. Knott, by defining with a very thick, rough brush the Circumference—not-Knott. Each of the chapters is a parabola without an apogee; the work as a whole is a circle without a center." [6] I would like to expand on this and show how Beckett, by applying the method of imitative form to other aspects of the book—in particular, narrative technique and archetypal patterning—puts the reader in Watt's very uncomfortable shoes.

Let us begin by looking at what Beckett has done to the business of narration.[7] We remarked in the last chapter that an important difference between the novel *Murphy* and the antinovel *More Pricks Than Kicks* was that the novel had point of view while the antinovel was trying hard to annihilate point of view. *Watt* represents a return in part to the effort in *More Pricks*. But the flights of parody, tonal shifts, and attacks on the conventional phrase which were so central to this task in the first book are now absorbed by a single recognizable voice. By comparison, their effects are considerably muted:

> As Watt came, so he went, in the night, that covers all things with its cloak, especially when the weather is cloudy. [P. 215]

> Now the fields flew by, the hedges and the ditches, ghastly in the train's light, or appeared to do so, for in reality it was the train that moved, across a land forever still. [P. 28]

The really pronounced stylistic departures are introduced by separate characters—Spiro, Arsene, Arthur. For a narrative voice, however, the author adopts a distinctive and carefully sustained style—what I have had occasion to call a "mean style." In this regard, at least, the book is more similar to *Murphy* than to *More Pricks*. But here the similarity ends; for Beckett has concentrated in *Watt* on extracting from his mean style all moral and emotional bias. What he has done can be shown by comparing the mean styles of *Murphy* and *Watt*:

> The sun shone, having no alternative, on the nothing new. Murphy sat out of it, as though he were free, in a mew in West Brompton. Here for what might have been six months he had eaten, drunk, slept, and put his clothes on and off, in a medium-sized cage of north-western aspect commanding an unbroken view of medium-sized cages of south-eastern aspect. Soon he would have to make other arrangements, for the mew had been condemned. Soon he would have to buckle to and start eating,

drinking, sleeping, and putting his clothes on and off, in quite alien surroundings.

Mr. Hackett turned the corner and saw, in the failing light, at some little distance, his seat. It seemed to be occupied. This seat, the property very likely of the municipality, or of the public, was of course not his, but he thought of it as his. This was Mr. Hackett's attitude towards things that pleased him. He knew they were not his, but he thought of them as his.

Perhaps the most noticeable difference is the absence in the second quotation of such pointer phrases as "having no alternative," "as though he were free," "a medium-sized cage," and "he would have to buckle to." The reader, in other words, is left without this network of ironic evaluative guides. But the basic difference between the styles is syntactical: "Mr. Hackett turned the corner and saw, in the failing light, at some little distance, his seat." It is the pacing of the sentence which attracts all the attention. A rhythm somewhere between that of music and that of automation, rather than a controlling personality, governs the flow of words. Later, when Watt becomes involved in his elaborate computations this quality becomes far more pronounced, and we have pages, as Kenner describes them, which "seem to have been written out in a trance of obligation, like some schoolroom imposition." [8] Kenner estimates that this may have derived from Joyce's exploitation of the catechism in chapter seventeen of *Ulysses*. This seems probable, though I think Joyce experimented with somewhat the same effect (and for similar reasons) throughout his novel: "Mr. Leopold Bloom ate with relish the inner organs of beast and fowl." Despite the obvious musical differences, the principle is the same. The syntax emphasizes an impersonal beat, so that the novel appears to create itself, carefully, patiently, breath by breath. And though, in *Watt*, monotony may be an easily acquired effect, the syntax is not without a great variety of rhythmic combinations. The effects that Beckett can achieve are often, to say the least, bizarre: "For when on Sam the sun shone bright, then in a vacuum panted Watt, and when Watt like a leaf was tossed, then stumbled Sam in deepest night" (p. 153).

But the general effect, to start with, is that of authorlessness. We have words under their own power, sentences unwinding according to mechanical principles uncontaminated by human origin. The effect, indeed, is akin to the "dramatic" quality sought by Joyce in *Ulysses*. What possible implicit metaphor a creator may be for a Creator is avoided by eliminating the evidence of the former. The reader, in short, is presented with an object in much the same way Watt is presented with the objects of his world. Whence came Mr. Knott? Is there a beginning to the cycles of his servants? How came his door to be open? The recurrent questions in the narrative are applicable to the narrative itself. Whence came this book? What is its significance? Or does it simply exist, detached from all causation?

In considering whether Beckett is in fact attempting to suggest complete authorlessness, complete absence of source or cause, it should be recalled just what kind of skeptic he is: "If there were only darkness, all would be clear. It is because there is not only darkness but also light that our situation becomes inexplicable." [9] Annihilating the sense of point of view, then, in order to imply an authorless world would constitute a kind of clarification. Beckett does not declaim that God is dead or that effects have no causes, just as he does not declaim the reverse. The problem is that we have, as we do in the paradigm of Mr. Knott's servants,

64

both senses always: of order and of absence of order, of darkness and light.

Thus Beckett does not, in fact, leave the book totally without authorial presence, but rather he compounds the mystery as to just how it was created, and by whom, and in what spirit. After reading seventy-nine pages of virtually authorless prose, the reader suddenly hears the narrator refer to himself. On page 153, he discovers, just as incidentally, that the narrator's name is Sam. This Sam is careful to point out several times that all he knows he learned from Watt. Yet there are things narrated which Watt could never have told Sam. So round and round it goes, like the voices in Watt's head —we are never sure whether they are coming from the inside or from the outside.

The effect is similar to that Beckett gained in *More Pricks Than Kicks* in the chapter entitled "Ding-Dong" when the narrative voice suddenly becomes the voice of a narrator. Yet in *Watt* there is a third narrative approach that overlays the other two. This is the author as editor—source of work unknown or unexplained. So the book is—not riddled, not even sprinkled—just marked at long intervals with the trappings of the form. We have, in a mild crescendo at the end, a series of hiatuses in the manuscript. We have the unintelligible words: "so   ?   when empty" (p. 29), "perhaps his blood was deficient in   ?   " (p. 32). (Or was the narrator simply at a loss for words? Or was Beckett, composing in some farmhouse at Roussillon in the Vaucluse, simply lacking dictionary and thesaurus?) We have footnotes, though these footnotes are often in the style of the narrative.

The worlds within worlds do not end here. The title page attributes the book to one Samuel Beckett. And whether we like it or not, the narrator imprisoned in the narrative is named Sam. Sam is a plodding, faithful reporter, though, as he says, "This does not mean either that I may not have left out some of the things that Watt told me, or foisted in others that Watt never told me, though I was most careful to note down all at the time, in my little notebook" (p. 126). Yet Sam suddenly blossoms into Samuel with the addenda at the end. Now the work is no longer reportage, but a contrived work of fiction—a project. Here is the craftsman's raw material: "*Watt learned to accept,* etc. Use to explain poverty of Part III" (p. 248). Yet, turning about again, what is Samuel's attitude toward his project? "The following precious and illuminating material should be carefully studied. Only fatigue and disgust prevented its incorporation" (p. 247n). Or is it Samuel?

Our experience, then, of the narrative process is an experience of mysteries of intention, causation, origin, significance. At the end of the book we read the perfectly devastating comment: "No symbols where none intended." It tells us everything and nothing. The mystery is locked in the phrase, compounded as it is of just the proper mix of light and dark. The experience is directly imitative of Watt's experience of even minute literal details in the narrative. He is, for example, plagued by the ringing that seems to come from Erskine's room. Who pressed the bell? How? And for what? How is Watt going to find out? Can he ask Erskine? Can he get into the room? Can he get the key? Can he pick the lock? After developing all these questions and more for eight pages, the author could well have left both Watt and the reader in utter darkness. But no, he provides us in the end with a scrap of light. Watt at last—"Ruse a by"—enters the room, and we at last discover that "there was a bell in Erskine's room, but it was broken" (p. 128). There are many, many other things in Erskine's room—each one a new source of wonder and bewilderment to Watt. But how that broken bell was caused to ring or whether in fact it was not that bell but another bell that rang we are never informed.

66

What is especially intriguing is the way the narrative has of sliding between hypothesis and "fact," leaving the reader with a very finely created awareness of a reality at once actual and hypothetical. In a sense it resembles "all the incidents of note proposed to Watt during his stay in Mr. Knott's house . . . and in a sense not" (p. 72). Perhaps the deftest handling of this ambiguity is the long passage devoted to the dogs-for-the-slops problem. It starts out as a problem—absurd to begin with and made more absurd by the exacting, finicky thoroughness (that is, almost thoroughness) of Watt's reasoning. Perhaps the reader can content himself at the beginning that he is simply observing a peculiar mind running rampant on a pseudo-problem. Why for that matter should the slops be eaten at all? But then, to his amazement, the reader finds himself in the actuality of the Lynch family. The modulation is so subtle that it is very hard to say where Watt's hypothesizing leaves off and fact begins. But Watt's deductions are very nearly correct, and here are Art and Con, the twin dwarfs to tell the tale.

To ease his frustration, the reader understandably steps back to gain a better view of the whole. He looks for some pattern that will yield a meaning. And it is almost inevitable, considering his bewilderment with the literal texture of the work, that he looks for allegory. Indeed, he will find much to work with: as Hesla writes, "every major scene and incident, seems to invite interpretation, whether plausible or not, based on esoteric intelligence." [10] And after locating in Watt's journey not only the seven stages of the cross but the pilgrimage into hell, Hesla notes: "The reader is driven to these and other interpretations of incidents in the novel because he suffers, like Watt, from an inability to discover any meaning, 'even the most literal,' in these incidents." [11] Yet this is where we must be careful. For Beckett is dealing with the sense of order coupled with the sense of its absence, and there is no better structural device for this—nothing more teasing to the pattern-minded—than the trappings of allegory. Hesla operates with considerable subtlety and awareness and does acknowledge that "there is too much in the novel which cannot be accounted for by reference to a neat allegorical system." [12] Yet, if I am right that Beckett is practicing imitative form in *Watt,* then considering his subject, the function, surely, of most of the allegorical elements will be precisely the reverse of traditional allegory—that is, to frustrate the search for meaning rather than to satisfy it. They put us again, in short, in the position of Watt.

This is not to say that Watt's journey does not quite genuinely correlate with Watt's deepening involvement in the ineffability of things. His moving attempts to communicate his experience of Knott in Part III certainly spring from the experience itself. This basic structural substance can be validly defined. But Beckett has overlaid this basic structure with a medley of traditional or archetypal patterns that are highly suggestive of allegory. And these generate in the reader the experience of system/asystem which Watt undergoes at the house of Mr. Knott.

Here are just a few of them.

1. *The Hero at First Seen Darkly:* The figure of the hero is shrouded in mystery at the outset, perceived through rumor or as a form moving in the distance or the shadows. Thus Ahab, Heathcliff, and Gatsby are endowed at the start with depth and importance. So, too, Watt is first seen at a distance—indeed at such a distance and in such darkness that it is hard to tell whether he is in fact "a parcel, a carpet for example, or a roll of tarpaulin, wrapped up in dark paper and tied about the middle with a cord" (p. 16). Slowly, with great effort, we piece together Watt's fascinating past: for example, seven years ago he borrowed six and nine-

pence from Goff Nixon to buy a boot. Yet the real mystery remains: why did he get off at "merely facultative stop"? He is on a journey, granted, but why did he stop here? Why did he not ride on? Or turn back once he got off? A dark mystery. Mr. Hackett is strangely obsessed by it, and, to make matters worse, he cannot explain why.

2. *The Religious Guides:* Spiro ("My friends call me Dum, . . . I am so bright and cheerful. D-U-M. Anagram of mud" [p. 27].) falls in the great tradition of Dante's Virgil and Sir Guyon's Pardoner. His lesson, preparing Watt for the trials of his quest, is on the rat (Watt's best friend in the animal kingdom): more particularly, matters relating to a rat's, or another small animal's, ingestion of "a consecrated wafer." Unfortunately, Watt does not hear this improving discourse because of other voices with which, "if he was not familiar, he was not unfamiliar either" (p. 29).

If Spiro is Watt's Virgil, Arsene is his Beatrice. Arsene's lesson is longer. Erskine, who is most uninformative, corresponds to the figure of Knowledge in *Everyman:* "And now for a little along the way that lies between you and me Erskine will go by your side, to be your guide, and then for the rest you will travel alone, or with only shades to keep you company" (p. 63).

3. *The Perilous Voyage:* Watt crashes to the station floor after colliding with a surly porter, just as, on his return, he is knocked senseless for awhile by the inswinging waiting-room door. More terrible than either of these is the threat of Lady McCann whose attack could well have proved fatal: "for had the stone fallen on an ear, or on the back of the neck, as it might so easily have done, as it so nearly did, why then a wound had perhaps been opened, never again to close, never, never again to close, for Watt had a poor healing skin, and perhaps his blood was deficient in   ?   "

(p. 32). The hero is nevertheless undaunted and, "faithful to his rule, took no more notice of this aggression than if it had been an accident" (p. 32).

4. *The Chapel Perilous:* The House of Holiness, the Dark Tower, the Castle of Perserverance: here Watt meets and serves Knott for a while. Knott is draped in religious allusion. He is a flux of appearances. He needs never to need and he needs to be witnessed. He says "tweet" and "plopf." He says "Exelmans!" and "Cavendish!" He has a gardener named Graves. He has a bad piano. He watches a worm and bird. He climbs a tree.

Watt cannot say just what this means.

5. *The Rejection from Paradise:* "He stood there, he remembered, with bowed head, and a bag in each hand, and his tears fell, a slow minute rain, to the ground, which had recently been repaired. He would not have believed such a thing possible, if he had not been there himself. The humidity thus lent to the road surface must, he reckoned, have survived his departure by as long as two minutes at least, if not three. Fortunately the weather was fine" (p. 208).

6. *The Fruits of the Journey:* This may have escaped critical notice: Watt no longer needs to urinate every hour. "This last regular link with the screen, for he did not count as such his weekly stool, nor biannual equinoctial nocturnal emission in vacuo, he now envisaged its relaxation, and eventual rupture, with sadness, and gladness, distinctly perceptible in an alternation of great rapidity, for some little time, and dying blurred together away, in due course" (pp. 232–233).

This is mock allegory in its most extreme form. It mocks not only the material but allegory itself. Further, to the extent that we have the "esoteric intelligence" Hesla speaks of, to that extent may we compound the mockery. This is not to imply by any means that such esoteric intelligence is of no value in reading *Watt*. On the contrary, it is by relying on such intelligence that Beckett achieves his effects; just as, in turn, it is Watt's intelligence that is the source of all his woe. The scholar, in other words, becomes a kind of super Watt. He becomes so, but for one singular advantage: he has a sense of humor. It is certainly time to note this, and to ackowledge the fact that the book is extremely funny.

It is, however, funny in a very different way from *Murphy*. Ruby Cohn observes this when she notes that Bergsonian theory, which could accommodate the earlier book, is no longer useful in talking about *Watt* for, as she says, "corrective and consolidating theories of comedy are irrelevant to Watt." [13] There are no longer properly speaking the butts of humor characteristic of *Murphy* and Bergsonian comedy in general, because there is no longer the distance required in such comedy so that we can speak of on the one hand a comic object and on the other hand an audience that laughs at it. We are, in short, too involved in Watt's predicament. As I have been arguing, the involvement is strongly abetted by imitative form: Watt's experiences are too much our own for us to laugh *at* him in the Bergsonian sense. But we do laugh.

In Arsene's long oration, he formulates a theory of humor, dividing the kinds of laughter into three types, which correspond to "successive excoriations of the understanding." The theory can be used to clarify what kind of laughter it is which is evoked by *Watt*.[14] The first two laughs Arsene defines are the "bitter" and the "hollow": "The bitter laugh laughs at that which is not good, it is the ethical laugh. The hollow laugh laughs at that which is not true, it is the intellectual laugh" (p. 48). They describe well the effects achieved in *Murphy* and *More Pricks*, respectively. In *Murphy* we laugh the bitter laugh. The objects of mirth are mirthful because they are not good: Miss Carridge, the plutomaniac caterers, the sane, Neary's love, Miss Counihan's stupidity. In *More Pricks*, and, more consistently, in "A Case in a Thousand," we laugh the hollow laugh. The objects of mirth are not a bad Dr. Nye and a bad Belacqua but false modes of fiction: ways of depicting existence which are not true.

Arsene defines the third laugh as "the dianoetic laugh, down the snout—Haw!—so. It is the laugh of laughs, the *risus purus,* the laugh laughing at the laugh, the beholding, the saluting of the highest joke, in a word the laugh that laughs—silence please—at that which is unhappy" (p. 48). In *Watt* as Josephine Jacobsen and William R. Mueller point out, we have certain outstanding examples of this kind of humor in the descriptions of the Lynch family and the unfortunate Mary who could never stop eating.[15] But surely the greatest source of unhappiness in the book is what it is about—the ineffability of things. And the greatest source of humor is the unhappy Watt, whose unhappiness is caused by this ineffability. The inability to express, the absence of meaning, the inability to understand are the dominant themes of Arsene's discourse. At the end, he circles back and weds his themes to the *risus purus:* "What we know partakes in no small measure of the nature of what has so happily been called the unutterable or ineffable, so that any attempt to utter or eff it is doomed to fail, doomed, doomed to fail. Why even I myself strolling all alone in some hard earned suspension of labour in this charming garden, have tried and tried to formulate this delicious haw!" (p. 62).

This is the effect—the haw! not the formulation— that Beckett was trying to achieve in *Watt.* The quest pattern with all its various archetypal parts brings a strong sense of importance that collides with the events in the narrative. When we learn that Watt no longer has to urinate every hour, or when we witness Lady McCann's attack, we laugh *at* neither the figures involved nor the quest pattern in which they are contained. We laugh in the face of an absence of meaning.

A crucial component in this technique, as well as others in the work, is the preestablished meaning in the mind of the reader: his intelligence, esoteric or otherwise. It is essential that the reader bring to *Watt* meanings that he associates with the quest pattern. For the mystery that Beckett is working with in *Watt* is not simply a mystery *in vacuo*—the experience of the blind man given sight. Rather it is a mystery arising from the constant violation of past meanings:

> Watt preferred on the whole having to do with things of which he did not know the name, though this too was painful to Watt, to having to do with things of which the known name, the proven name, was not the name, anymore, for him. For he could always hope, of a thing of which he had never known the name, that he would learn the name, some day, and so be tranquillized. But he could not look forward to this in the case of a thing of which the true name has ceased, suddenly, or gradually, to be the true name for Watt. [Pp. 81–82]

As I have been arguing, Watt and the reader are in the same predicament. There is only one major difference—the reader has a sense of humor. This is crucial, for humor has become a key effect in Beckett. Watt is so deficient in this faculty that he can barely smile—and this only with discomfort. Afflicted with the greatest agony in Beckett's *Weltanschauung*—the inability to understand, the inability to express, together with the obligation to express—Watt becomes a very unhappy man. He must "weigh absence in a scale," exorcise the mystery, find his "pillow of old words."

Laughter is the lesson of *Watt*. Without laughter—it is an old lesson—one goes mad. Through it one experiences and accepts the mystery. "In the beginning was the pun"; [16] and as everyone knows, one cannot spell out a joke. There is no spelling out *Watt*. One laughs —neither at what is bad nor at what is false—but to accommodate the mystery.

4

Reaction

Mercier et Camier was composed shortly after *Watt* in 1946, though Beckett has only recently allowed its publication. Two innovations most clearly distinguish it from the earlier writing. They are not part of my subject but are worth taking note of before we proceed. The first is its composition in French. When asked why he abandoned his native language, Beckett has usually been rather coy. Numerous hypotheses exist on the subject,[1] but the possibility also exists that the switch in languages may in part be an effect of his experiences in writing *Watt*. The second innovation is the use of a couple (or "pseudocouple" as it is called in *The Unnamable*). This innovation led in turn to a good deal of dialogue. Indeed, Mercier and Camier are so talkative that their dialogue continues in their sleep. "Mais ce sera par l'effet du hasard," the author comments, and adds, "Mais se sont-ils jamais parlé autrement?" (pp. 180–181).[2] Much of this dialogue is brilliant comedy, and there is no doubt that it helped prepare the way for *Godot*.[3] Again, this turn from the inner space of a single mind to the much more consistently external presentation of a chattering dyad may be a rather direct "consequence" of *Watt*.

I suggest this possibility because what Beckett appears to be doing in *Mercier et Camier* is seeking some quite new combination of effects. From the point of view of the literary craftsman, it is a trial balloon, an exploratory work, a workshop—as well as an amusement. What I wish to show are aspects of this experimentation which represent an attempt to release it from the disintegration imminent in *Watt*. My inference is that at this stage of his career—before the trilogy—Beckett could see no further step that could be taken successfully in the direction he had gone in *Watt*.[4] Yet at the same time he was not willing to step all the way back to *Murphy*, though, and indeed for this reason, Janvier's phrase for *Murphy*—"ce livre nerveux"—is also appropriate for *Mercier et Camier*. It is a work curiously, gently, at odds with itself. In contrast to *Watt*, it is an experiment in coherence. It represents, likewise, no significant development of imitative form. Yet it does retain a number of disintegrative, antinovelistic devices—efforts at frustrating the reader's sense of closure—particularly in the spheres of plot and characterization. Let us start, then, with these and follow up with the ways the book resists confusion.

The story is about the journey of a "grand barbu," Mercier, and a "petit gros," Camier. Actually, it is about the failure of that journey. They are, as Mercier puts it "empêtré dans une histoire sans issue." Most of the time is spent in a labyrinthine city named Bondy[5] where Mercier and Camier either prepare to depart, or prepare to prepare to depart, or return, or get lost, or get separated, or get reunited. Twice they manage to leave. The first time they take the train a short way south to a small village and even manage to go beyond the village to a countryside unique in its desolation. The second time they seem to go farther. They penetrate a high, vast region of bogs and ruins, devoid of humanity, with panoramas of sea and mountains. The end of the book finds them back in the city on the bank of a canal where they part for the last time.

Causes for their failure are numerous. They are, to begin with, thwarted by a "longue série d'êtres malfaisants," including one hotel manager, one tavern manager, and several guardians of the law, one of whom they kill. Their progress is also interrupted by a variety of bars where they pause for refreshment and by several layovers at the house of their friend Hélène. Moreover, they are handicapped, as one might guess, by their incompetence. They attach great importance to their few possessions—a bicycle, a raincoat, a parasol, a sack—which are, sometimes rationally, sometimes not so rationally, necessary for their voyage but which they continually lose, destroy, or reject.[6] Frailty of both memory and sense of direction are influential here. Finally, there is the rather significant problem that the goal of their journey is a total mystery to them. Some shreds of enlightenment may be available in their sack, but then the whereabouts of their sack is also a mystery. All they are really certain of is the necessity of making the trip. "Une seule chose comptait: partir. . . . Et puis merde."

Like the other books, *Mercier et Camier* is a fraud. Beckett accentuates the imposture. He manipulates the elements of setting, character, and incident in the manner of an author seeking relief from the somehow necessary task of manipulating those very elements. Scenes open with a setting provided as if on cue. The setting grows, burgeons, until the author can stand it no more and characters are introduced. "Fin du paysage descriptif," he remarks at one point, abruptly turning to his protagonists. The latter in turn soon evoke that air of resigned sarcasm with which we are by now well familiar. In middialogue he intrudes: "Ce jeu-là ne durera pas longtemps." And later, despairing: "Que tout cela est lamentable." Then, often, he will revert back to the setting for diversion. His specialty is rainy landscapes at nightfall. These he charges with sham profundity and mordant lyricism (a combination that he continued to develop through *Texts for Nothing*).

When neither protagonists nor setting provide relief, secondary characters are thrust into the narrative. Madden and Monsieur Conaire announce themselves and their plights in the gusty rhetoric that Pozzo and Hamm will later use in their set pieces: "à voix haute et dans le style noble que je haïs," as Madden describes it. Their storms of eloquence underline the gratuitousness of their presence. In a small hotel in a small village south of Bondy where, entirely by chance, Mercier and Camier spend the night, Monsieur Conaire makes his thundering entrance. He is dressed in riding breeches and alpine boots and carries a heavy sack and a huge staff. "Vous voyez devant vous, Messieurs . . . un homme. Profitez-en," he announces to the manager and the barman:

> Je suis venu à pied du plus profond du four à gaz métropolitain, sans m'arrêter une suele fois, sauf pour—. Il regarda autour de lui, vit Thérèse . . . se pencha pardessus le comptoir et acheva sa phrase à voix basse. Ses yeux allaient de monsieur Gast à Georges (le barman s'appelle maintenant Georges), de Georges à monsieur Gast, comme pour s'assurer que ses paroles avaient produit l'effet escompté. Puis se redressant il dit d'une voix sonore, Peu et souvent, peu et souvent, et lentement, lentement, voilà où j'en suis. Il lança un coup d'oeil vers Thérèse et partit d'un rire strident. Il avait réussi une plainsanterie entre hommes. [Pp. 78–79]

> [I have come on foot from the very depths of the metropolitan oven, without stopping once, except to—. He looked around, saw Thérèse . . . leaned over the counter and whispered, his eyes went from Monsieur Gast to Georges (the barman is now called Georges), from Georges to Monsieur Gast, as if to make sure that his words had produced the desired effect. Then, straightening up, he said in a sonorous voice, Briefly and often, briefly and

78

often, and slowly, slowly, that's what I've come to. He glanced at Therese and burst into shrill laughter. He had brought off a joke among men.] [7]

Why has he come? To meet a certain Camier who we learn to our infinite surprise is a private detective. Camier fails to keep his appointment because he and Mercier are already asleep. And when he meets M. Conaire the following day, he tells him coldly: "J'avais compris, ou plutôt décidé, que mon travail était fini, je veux dire le travail qu'on me connaît, et que j'avais eu tort en pensant que vous pourriez vous joindre à nous, même pour un jour ou deux" (p. 104). So much for Monsieur Conaire.

It is also in *Mercier et Camier* that Beckett begins to develop in earnest his ghostly technique of transplanting characters, or at least names, from earlier fiction. When Mercier and Camier first arrive at the hotel mentioned above, they are greeted by a manager whom Mercier immediately recognizes as a common figure in his dreams. "Il y a longtemps que votre personne me hante," he tells him, "Vous vous tenez généralement sur un seuil, ou à une fenêtre. Derrière vous un torrent de lumière et de joie, qui devrait normalement réduire vos traits à néant" (p. 66). He even knows his name—Monsieur Gall, thus recalling the piano tuner who haunted the mind of Watt. As it turns out, the manager is not named Gall. He is rather (and appropriately) Monsieur Gast. Present also in this scene is a M. Graves who evokes, at least in name, the memory of Mr. Knott's gardener. Yet more astonishing than either of these is Watt himself who dramatically appears in the last chapter. He is totally transformed: swaggering, talkative, whiskey-drinking, though, as it shortly turns out, quite violently mad. He is, he admits, "méconnaissable," but predicts that one day he will be better known, though not universally: "il y a peu de chances

par example que ma notoriété pénètre jusqu'aux habi-
tants de Londres ou de Cuq-Toulza" (p. 193). He
claims to have known Camier from birth, while Mercier
says that he resembles one Murphy who died ten years
ago under mysterious circumstances.

One should not leave this part of the argument without including some examples of the dialogue, for it is
in this that Beckett's gifts for comic confusion show to
best advantage. My first example comes from chapter
one. Mercier and Camier have entered a shelter to
keep out of the rain. Present also in the shelter are two
dogs, copulating, and as we later learn, a bicycle. The
bicycle emerges mysteriously. Mercier and Camier did
not arrive with it, yet they take it with them when they
go. An ominous and uniformed caretaker suddenly appears:

> A qui est cette bicyclette? dit-il.
> Mercier et Camier se regardèrent.
> Nous n'avions pas besoin de ça, dit Camier.
> Enlevez-la, dit le gardien.
> Ce serait peut-être une petite distraction, dit
> Mercier.
> A qui sont ces chiens? dit le gardien.
> Pour moi, dit Camier, nous allons être obligés
> de nous éloigner.
> Serait-ce le coup de fouet dont nous avions
> besoin, pour nous mettre en route? dit Mercier.
> M'obligerez-vous à appeler un agent? dit le
> gardien.
> On dirait qu'il sent mauvais, par dessus le
> marché, dit Camier.
> Préférez-vous que j'appelle un serrurier, dit le
> gardien, pour qu'il fracture le cadenas? Ou que
> je l'enlève moi-même, à coups de pied dans les
> rayons?
> Comprends-tu quelque chose à ces propos in-
> cohérents? dit Camier.

Ma vue a beaucoup baissé, dit Mercier. Il est question, je crois, d'une bicyclette.

Et alors? dit Camier.

Sa présence ici, dit Mercier, serait contraire à la loi.

Alors, qu'il l'enlève, dit Camier.

Il ne peut pas, dit Mercier. Un système de sûreté quelconque, tel un cadenas, ou un câble, l'attache, à un arbre sans doute, ou à une statue. Telle est du moins mon interprétation.

Elle est plausible, dit Camier.

Malheureusement il n'y a pas que la bicyclette, si j'ai bien compris, dit Mercier. Il y a aussi les chiens.

Que font-ils de mal? dit Camier.

Ils contreviennent à l'arrêté, dit Mercier, au même titre que la petite reine.

Mais eux ils ne sont attachés à rien, dit Camier, sinon l'un à l'autre, par le coït.

Cela est vrai, dit Mercier. [Pp. 19–21]

[Whose bicycle is this? he said.

Mercier and Camier looked at each other.

We didn't need this, said Camier.

Remove it, said the caretaker.

It may provide some amusement, said Mercier.

Whose dogs are these? said the caretaker.

If you ask me, said Camier, we shall be obliged to leave.

Could this be what we've needed to set us on our way? said Mercier.

Will I have to call a policeman? said the caretaker.

On top of that he seems to smell bad, said Camier.

Or do you want me to call a locksmith, said the caretaker, to break the padlock? Or would you rather I removed it myself by kicking in the spokes?

Can you make anything of this blather? said Camier.

I don't see as well as I used to, said Mercier. It concerns a bicycle, I believe.

So? said Camier.

Its presence here, said Mercier, seems to be against the law.

Then let him remove it, said Camier.

He can't, said Mercier. Some kind of fastening device, like a padlock or cable, secures it to a tree, no doubt, or a statue. Such at least is my interpretation.

It sounds plausible, said Camier.

Unfortunately there is not only the bicycle, if I understand correctly, said Mercier. There are the dogs as well.

What are they doing wrong? said Camier.

They are transgressing the law, said Mercier, in the same way as the bike.

But they aren't secured to anything, said Camier, except to each other by coitus.

That's true, said Mercier.]

One could describe the thrust of this dialogue as outward. That is, the mysteries that arise have to do with law and the social order, represented in the person of the caretaker and the regulation concerning the bicycle. The following dialogue forms a good contrast. Its interest lies in the other direction, for the mysteries that arise have to do with the purpose and direction of Mercier and Camier themselves. Again, the vehicle is a simple object:

Je suis prêt à tout essayer, dit Mercier, à condition de savoir quoi.

82

Nous allons donc rentrer bien gentiment, et sans nous dépêcher, en ville, dit Camier, et y rester le temps qu'il faudra.

Le temps qu'il faudra pour quoi faire? dit Mercier.

Pour récupérer les objets que nous avons égarés, dit Camier, ou pour y renoncer.

Il a dû en effet être riche en finesses, dit Mercier, le raisonnement capable de nous amener à une décision pareille.

Il me semble, dit Camier, quoique je ne puisse le certifier, que le sac est le noeud de toute cette affaire. Nous avons décidé, je crois, qu'il s'y trouve, ou s'y trouvait, un ou plusieurs objets dont nous pouvons difficilement nous passer.

Mais nous avons déjà passé en revue tout ce qu'il contenait, dit Mercier, et jugé qu'il n'y avait là que du superflu.

Je ne le nie pas, dit Camier, et il est peu probable que notre conception du superflu se soit modifié, depuis hier matin. D'où vient donc notre trouble? Voilà la question que nous avons dû nous poser.
[Pp. 93–94]

[I am ready to try anything, said Mercier, on condition that I know what it is.

We shall return then, like good little boys, and without haste, to the city, said Camier, and stay there as long as it takes.

As long as it takes to do what? said Mercier.

To recover the objects which we have misplaced, said Camier, or to abandon them.

The reasoning capable of leading us to such a decision, said Mercier, must indeed have been rich in subtleties.

It seems to me, said Camier, though I cannot prove it, that the sack is the crux of this affair. We concluded, I think, that it contains, or contained, one or several objects which it would be difficult to do without.

But we have already reviewed everything that it contained, said Mercier, and decided that there was nothing there but superfluity.

I don't deny that, said Camier, and it is hardly probable that our conception of superfluity should have changed since yesterday morning. What, then, is the source of our confusion? That is the question we should have asked ourselves.]

The fictional methods we have been reviewing constitute ample demonstration that Beckett has not abandoned his literary subject, or object, in *Mercier et Camier*. And yet it is my contention that Beckett does not go to the depth of confusion here which he achieved in *Watt* and later will achieve in the trilogy. As I suggested at the beginning of this chapter, Beckett appears to be toying with methods by which to resist complete formal disintegration. These methods generally are one of two types—a return to conventional fiction and an arbitrary use of symmetrical patterning.

To observe the first type let us turn to the brutal murder that Mercier and Camier commit. For our purposes this is an especially important event because both Molloy and Moran commit similar brutal acts. The contrast between the latter deeds and those of Mercier and Camier is sharp, and it lies in this: Mercier and Camier are motivated by a rational, or at least understandable, cause. They are responding, if you will, to police brutality. The policeman is causing Camier a great deal of pain. Mercier comes to Camier's aid, and when Camier is released he gives vent to his rage by revenging himself on the policeman. Still more worthy of note is the way the policeman is described as he warms to the task of belaboring Camier:

Cela commençait à l'intéresser. Ce n'était pas tous les jours qu'un divertissement de cette qualité venait rompre le monotonie de sa faction. Le métier avait du bon, il l'avait toujours dit. Il sortit son batôn. Allez, hop, dit-il, et pas d'histoires. [P. 157]

[This began to interest him. It wasn't every day that a diversion of this sort occurred to break the montony of his beat. His job wasn't so bad; he had always said so. He pulled out his nightstick. Step on it, he said, and shut up.]

This is conventional satiric description. It is quite similar to satiric modes employed so freely in *Murphy*. The caretaker in chapter one is described with the same relish:

Son uniforme, vert d'un vert détrempé et copieuse-ment garni, à l'endroit réglementaire, d'insignes héroïques et de rubans, lui allait bien, très bien. Fort de l'example du grand Sarsfield, il avait failli crever dans la défense d'un territoire qui en lui-même devait certainement le laisser indifférent et qui considéré comme symbole ne l'excitait pas beaucoup non plus probablement. [Pp. 17–18]

[His uniform, a sodden green in color and copi-ously garnished in the official place with heroic insignia and ribbons, became him well, very well. True to the example of the great Sarsfield, he had almost died in the defense of a territory which in itself surely must not have mattered to him and which as a symbol didn't excite him much either probably.]

85

One can find other examples. M. Gast, though his character is somewhat more slippery, is essentially a petit-bourgeois:

> Ils ont payé? dit monsieur Gast.
> Oui, dit le barman.
> C'est tout ce qui m'intéresse, dit monsieur Gast.
> Ils ne me disent rien qui vaille, dit le barman.
> Surtout le grand barbu. Le petit gros, ça va encore.
> Ne t'occupe pas de ça, dit monsieur Gast. [P. 74]

When Watt begins to grow violent in the last chapter, another manager is introduced. He is dressed in pearl grey trousers and yellow shoes. "Comme boutonniere il avait choisi une tulipe." Mercier and Camier, by dint of fast-talking, convince him that he should allow them to remain.

> Calmez-le, dit le gérant. Ne m'obligez pas à sévir. Il se retira. Il avait été ferme sans raideur, humain avec dignité, il saurait se justifier auprès de ses habitués, bouchers pour la plupart, que la mort de l'agneau avait rendus un peu intolérants. [P. 202]

> [Calm him down, said the manager. Do not oblige me to be severe. He withdrew. He had been firm without rigidity, humane with dignity, he would be able to justify himself to his regular customers, butchers for the most part, whom the death of the lamb had left a little intolerant.]

Such clearly etched satirical portraits are not to be found in *Watt* and are clearly quite different from such strange presences as Madden and Conaire. Like the satirical parts of *Murphy*, they point to a "real" world and impart much of the solidity commonly associated with the traditional novel. A key factor here is the con-

86

sistent third person narration that Beckett sustains from beginning to end. Granted, he is somewhat mystifying when he claims in his very first sentence that he can tell this story because he was with Mercier and Camier the whole time. But I believe Kenner is right in interpreting this as a reference to "his continual invisible presence . . . [as] creator and puppet master." [8] Indeed, the important point is that he *is* continually present, lending a sense, at least, of authorial management which is in sharp contrast with the bewildering tricks played in *Watt* and the variety of authorial postures assumed in *More Pricks Than Kicks*.

In this way, Beckett maintains a consistent exteriority in the image of life presented. It is this that lends itself to the satire discussed above. It also lends itself to the various delineation of incidental life that is the stuffing of a traditional novel:

> Ils montaient pour la plupart dans de vieilles Fords hautes sur roue. D'aucuns s'éparpillaient par le village, à la recherche d'occasions. D'autres enfin se mettaient à causer par petits groupes, sous la pluie, dont ils ne semblaient nullement gênés. . . . Bientôt ils seraient loin, dispersés par les chemins qu'efface avidement déjà le crépuscule du jour avare. Chacun se hâte vers son petit royaume, vers sa femme qui attend, vers ses bêtes bien au chaud, vers ses chiens à l'affût du moteur du maître. [Pp. 74–75]

> [Most of them climbed into old high-sprung Fords. Some scattered through the village in search of bargains. Others drifted into small groups to talk, in the rain, which didn't seem to bother them at all. . . . Soon they would be far away, dispersed on roads already being swallowed up by the twilight of a niggardly day. Each hastens toward his little kingdom, toward his waiting spouse, his snug

animals, his dogs lying in wait for the master's car.]

More important still, Beckett keeps us on the outside of his two central characters. Only once are we allowed to enter and observe at any length the hubbub within a single mind. (The mind is Mercier's "où passé et avenir se confondaient d'une façon peu agréable, et où présent tenait la rôle ingrat de noyé éternal.") [9] The interior voice that plagues Watt and later narrators is only acknowledged in passing:

> La petite voix implorante, dit Camier, qui nous parle parfois de vies antérieures, la connais-tu?
> Je la confonds de plus en plus, dit Mercier, avec celle qui veut me faire croire que je ne suis pas encore mort. Mais je vois ce que tu veux dire. [P. 94]

> [The little imploring voice, said Camier, which tells us at times of previous existences—are you familiar with it?
> I confound it more and more, said Mercier, with the one which tries to convince me I am not yet dead. But I see what you mean.]

We are not, as we are in *Watt* and *Molloy,* immersed in the bafflement of a single mind. And though we are certainly baffled by our protagonists, we are generally a secure distance from them. They are essentially flat. It is not surprising that when Beckett again devised a couple, he accentuated this flatness by placing it in the hard visual clarity of the stage.

One can also speak of a geographical control in this book—again, in comparative terms. We, of course, never have a coherent map of the city in our minds, but it does act as a headquarters with certain fixed properties—the canal, Hélène's—which we return to. The first excursion takes us south of this city a short way. In the second excursion, when we seem to have gone farther, the city is still visible far below on the edge of the sea. Time, in turn, seems to proceed regularly, chronologically, for about two weeks. The contrast again is sharp with the books immediately before and after.

As I suggested, these techniques tend to pull the book back in the direction of *Murphy*. But the other side of Beckett's "experimentation with coherence" tends to pull the book forward—toward *How It Is*. I call this an arbitrary use of symmetrical patterning, and the term to stress is "arbitrary," for the effect is that of sheer gratuitousness. It is noticeable in the regularity with which events recur—the parasol, Hélène, bars, policemen, managers—or in the symmetrical form of the travels themselves with their two balancing excursions and their conclusion near the spot where they began. It is also noticeable in the book's system of rainy nightfalls. Rain dominates the book from beginning to end, but in almost every chapter Beckett halts the narrative to describe that mysterious hour when a dark afternoon gives way to night. But far and away the most strikingly symmetrical feature of the book is Beckett's curious chapter arrangement. Of the book's twelve chapters, every third constitutes a break, dividing the book into four sections of two chapters each. These third chapters (3, 6, 9, 12) are simply résumés of the two preceding chapters. These résumés, in turn are simply lists of words and phrases which evoke the sequence of events in a chapter. The effect is that of a container, or grid, which provides a mathematical form to which the material must yield. Writing the book, then, becomes a kind of game of ordering. The author, for reasons unknown, is given the onerous task of recording the strange adventures of Mercier and Camier. Yet to sweeten the task, to give it the challenge of a game, he is provided with a form in which these adventures must be contained. When the form ends, the book ends.

It is in this way especially that the book appears as Kenner describes it: "an amusement of its creator, an amusement fiercely pursued." [10] Where in *Watt* (another four-part work) one has the sense of a constant and doomed effort to order things, in *Mercier et Camier* one has the sense of an order established handily and implacably. The order in the latter book, as I say, is gratuitous and it may have been Beckett's purpose to provide an order of such mathematical clarity that it would enlarge by contrast the mystery it contained. Yet Beckett's playful experimentation with symmetry dominates this book. In one of the chapter résumés, one finds what constitutes a feeble protest against this domination: "Le cul et la chemise, avec graphiques (passage entièrement supprimé)" (p. 163). Yet the grid remains, essentially undisturbed. Later, in *Godot* and *Molloy*, the abstract, symmetrical elements are much more radically accentuated. Yet in these works, they fail to dominate because they are far better integrated with elements of disorder and subjected to a fine and continuous series of disruptions.

This is a delightful book, yet there are several good reasons why an author like Beckett, who once called it "a dreadful book" [11] and who keeps such a watchful eye on the integrity of his canon, should have resisted for so long letting it appear in print. In fact, I would suspect that the book was undertaken without any real intention of having it published. Beckett was clearly using it to test the potential of a variety of different formal strategies. My working hypothesis has been that he did so in order to avoid the total collapse of form imminent in *Watt*. What resulted might in fact be described as a postponement of that collapse. But whatever one's hypothesis, it is highly probable that *Mercier et Camier* is not so much the effort of an author who is confused or of several minds about what he is doing as it is simply an effort to carry out a variety of simultaneous exercises. Thus he uses a new language, extends certain disintegrative techniques, revives conventions from *Murphy*, tests out the couple before *Godot*, and experiments with the kind of symmetricality so prevalent in the work of the sixties.

It may, however, simply have been the lightness of the work, as Fletcher estimates, that kept it out of print: "it did not strike the same hard note of solitude as the *Nouvelles*." [12] Certainly it is the *Nouvelles* that lead most directly to the trilogy. *Mercier et Camier* could well have been what it appears to be: an amusement, the kind of pastime perhaps that the later narrators find themselves so desperately in need of. For all its comic brilliance and subtlety, there is a simple, almost elementary, quality about it. This will become clearer in retrospect when we discuss *Malone Dies*, yet another child of *Mercier et Camier*, but one who inherited almost exclusively the formal potential of amusement and play. What results is richer than the earlier work both in complexity and integration, and comes closer to the balance Beckett was trying to achieve.

5

Two Reports

BEFORE THEY PART for the last time, Mercier turns to Camier and asks, "Tu te rapelles le perroquet?" And Camier replies, "Je me rappelle la chèvre." The exchange provides a critical yield, two animals rescued from the deluge. In the face of such "great formal brilliance and indeterminable import" one returns with a mixture of relief and despair to the parrot and the goat (though we are never sure whether Hélène's bird is in fact a parrot).[1] One is tempted to respond in the same way to *Molloy*, an altogether darker, denser, richer work with a symmetricality complicated by a more unyielding disorder. One remembers a stone and perhaps an orange Pomeranian.

The choice seems to be, for us as well as for Beckett, between saying little and saying a great deal. In general, criticism has chosen the latter alternative. In 1952, only a year after the publication of *Molloy*, Maurice Nadeau could write:

> It has been heaped with praise and learned comment, and such diverse meanings have been attributed to it that the more people talk about it the more obscure it seems. One person sees it as a masterpiece of humor, another as an epic of disaster. To some it is silence translated into words, to others no more than a literary exposition of complexes belonging more properly to psychoanalysis. In fact, everyone sees in it what he wants to see,

which is proof at once of the book's richness and
of its ambiguity.[2]

The years that followed have been similarly productive.
Yet despite our temptation at times to get back to the
stone and the Pomeranian, the research on *Molloy* has
not been by any means unfruitful. Scholarly digging is
very much in order, for much the same reason as it is
in *Watt*. Molloy is thick with allusions and parallels.
Hermes, Odysseus, Aeneas, Christ, Christian, Yahweh,
and Otto Rank are all present in one form or another,
providing ironic density for the mysteries the work at-
tends.

Furthermore, *Molloy* considerably amplifies the thematic richness of *Watt*. The main difference between
these two works is that attention has shifted from the
world of appearances to the world of the self. But we
are not, therefore, rid of the world of appearances or
Watt's baffling epistemological problems. We have, as
it were, a panorama of contingent mysteries radiating
from the core mystery of self; mysteries, that is, of the
nature and value of appearances, being, mind, corpo-
reality, love, birth, death, desire, and expression. Such
richness can certainly tolerate a variety of thematic interpretations.

But *Molloy* is also mined, as it were, with an equal
variety of perils to interpretation. A particularly obvious
example is the temptation it offers for a traditional psy-
choanalytical approach. The approach is tempting since
Molloy is ostensibly seeking, of all things, his mother.
His quest takes the shape of an outrageous parody of
Freudian allegory. Yet the parody *is* outrageous, and
this is the point to stress. His mother is a "deaf blind
impotent mad old woman, who called me Dan and
whom I called Mag" (p. 19)[3] and who probably confused Molloy with his father. He remembers her head
best: "Veiled with hair, wrinkles, filth, slobber" (p. 19).
He communicated with her—and that barely—by rap-

ping on her skull. And he forgives her for having "jostled me a little in the first months and spoiled the only endurable, just endurable period of my enormous history" (p. 18). There is no doubt that Beckett is counting on our Freudian intelligence, but the end to which it is employed is not the same as would satisfy the Freudian interpreter. For any trauma, which for the analyst would explain a human disorder, would by its very existence compound the mystery Beckett is concerned with. His questioning, in other words, takes up where Freud's leaves off. What is needed, then, is the proper application of our Freudian intelligence to appreciate the book. The danger, as in *Watt*, lies in a strict allegorical reading that establishes coherence and in so doing tends to annihilate the mystery that Beckett is trying to convey through imitative form.

The problem is compounded by the fact that there *are* a number of limited and interpretable emblems within the narrative. But in addition to these, Beckett has also, as in *Watt*, employed a medley of archetypal patterns calculated to tempt a host of allegorists other than the Freudian. Moreover, the temptations are considerably more seductive in *Molloy* than in *Watt*. The effect, for example, of recognizing a common medieval motif in the forest transformation undergone by Molloy and Moran is quite different from that of our recognizing, say, the religious guide in Spiro or the dragon at the gates in Lady McCann. To begin with, there is a difference in tone arising from the fact that *Molloy* is narrated in the first person, while Watt is viewed from a distance. In addition, the sequence gains resonance by being repeated in both reports with the inclusion in both of the meeting and assault on the stranger. Through parallelism, a weight of importance is generated in the work itself, amplifying our feeling that we are in the presence of some profound meaning. Furthermore, and certainly most important, there is the sense of a vital transformation that goes with the forest (Lady McCann was not a significant threat and Spiro was not a significant guide).

What, however, is the nature of the transformation? The archetype suggests a discovery of self. There is no need denying this. Moran, in fact, makes it quite explicit that this is what is happening. The formulation is simply inadequate. The question still remains. For the term "self" is merely another name our protagonists love and dread. "And to tell the truth I not only knew who I was, but I had a sharper and clearer sense of my identity than ever before, in spite of its deep lesions and the wounds with which it was covered. And from this point of view I was less fortunate than my other acquaintances. I am sorry if this last phrase is not so happy as it might be. It deserved, who knows, to be without ambiguity" (p. 170).

What is this identity that emerges? Does Moran become Molloy as his decay in physique and appearance would suggest? Is it the Molloy he stalks within him, one of five Molloys he enumerates at the outset? If so, what is Molloy? And what does Molloy become in his turn on his quest—his mother? ("I must resemble her more and more. All I need now is a son" [p. 7].) Or is, perhaps, the voice Moran begins to hear his self? Then who is doing the listening? And who, then, is Youdi?

Beckett deliberately forestalls synthesis of these elements, thus generating in us the anxiety and enchantment of his narrators, who, like us, are struggling to order their material. In contrast, we have the structured self of Moran before his journey which can easily be defined in terms of his known world of limits. He is a bourgeois. We know him by his religion and his dress, by his attitudes toward his son, his housekeeper, his neighbors, and his beer. But with the abandonment of that structure comes the abandonment of definition. And it is imperative that the reader feel this. Beckett's method is to put us in the position of Moran immediately after the assault in the woods—cursed by a plenitude of keys. Moran struggles painfully to retrieve them and, once he has found as many as he can (but not all), he puts them together on a broken key ring.

Beckett's use of allusion in *Molloy* differs in no fundamental way from his use of it in *Watt*. *Molloy*, however, is distinguished not only from *Watt* but from the intervening work as well by two radical formal departures: the division into two parts and the narrative device of the report. This chapter will focus on these two innovations since both represent very important tactics in Beckett's renewed experimentation with imitative form.

One of the things Molloy steals from Lousse is a small silver object composed of two identical right-angle crosses joined at their intersections by a bar. It looks like this:

It is doubtless a knife-rest. But to Molloy it has no discernible function, for which very reason he is fascinated with it:

> I could never bring myself to sell it, even in my worst need, for I could never understand what possible purpose it could serve, nor even contrive the faintest hypothesis on the subject. And from time to time I took it from my pocket and gazed upon it, with an astonished and affectionate gaze, if I had not been incapable of affection. But for a certain time I think it inspired me with a kind of veneration, for there was no doubt in my mind that it was not an object of virtu, but that it had a most specific function always to be hidden from me. [Pp. 63–64]

Much later, in another book, in a story within a story, it reappears for an instant before disappearing again, perhaps for good. This is when Malone's creation Macmann is taken into the House of Saint John of God and "a little silver knife-rest" is found among his belongings (p. 258). It is the only one of his possessions which the attendants deem of sufficient value to preserve.

I am tempted to see in its symmetrical form the simplest paradigm of order: that very action should have its equal and opposite reaction; every effect, its cause; every object, its image; every crime, its fitting punishment. It is thus apropriate that Molloy, with his mania for symmetry, cannot bring himself to sell it. As he says: "I think it inspired me with a kind of veneration, for there was no doubt in my mind . . . that it had a most specific function always to be hidden from me."

Before Molloy introduces us to his mother, he produces the knife-rest's counterimage, A and C. They are first presented to us, lettered, together in the same setting. They "looked alike," Molloy says, both wearing greatcoats and together the only moving objects in the scene. Moving toward each other, they eventually descend into the same trough and there meet. Momentarily they are together, a couple. They exchange a few words. They "knew each other perhaps." Then the couple dissolves, the one going on toward town, the other into the country. Their parting breaks the single gestalt, and we find ourselves almost immediately considering, not one scene, but two separate individuals. Molloy dwells at length first on one, then on the other; as he does so the differences between them become more and more insistent. The one walks with uncertain step, unsure of where he is going; the other walks confidently toward town. The one wears a hat, a cocked hat, and carries a heavy stick; the other is hatless, wears sandshoes, smokes a cigar. He is a gentleman. He even has an orange Pomeranian. At one point he goes so far as to take the cigar from his lips and bury his face in the orange fleece. As I say, the discrete details become more and more insistent. The two letters, which Molloy had assigned them when they were part of the same scene, become confused. At last he entertains the possibility that he is "confusing several different occasions": "And perhaps it was A one day at one place, then C another at another, then a third the rock and I, and so on for the other components, the cows, the sky, the sea, the mountains" (p. 14). This is scenic description in reverse. Instead of building up a coherent tableau from a variety of well-selected impressions, Molloy allows us a fleeting glimpse of the tableau before resolving it into a collection of wholly separate bits, some patently imaginary. "He buried his face in the orange fleece." What are we to do with this? Perhaps, as Molloy implies, he was in love with the dog. This could very well be, but once we have progressed this far can we ever get back? Will it assist us at all in comprehending the tableau of A and C, or its significance?

The whole fiasco of A and C is developed between a first start ("Here's my beginning. . . . Here it is" [p. 8]) and a second ("having waked between eleven o'clock and midday . . . I resolved to go and see my mother" [p. 15]). It is preamble, a seven-page epitome of the mysteries of relation that are to baffle our voyagers: Molloy's behavior and the policeman's response, the charcoal-burner's behavior and Molloy's response, Molloy and his mother, Molloy and Moran, their minds and their bodies, their pasts and the written records thereof, the punishment they endure and the sin that brought it on (that of having been born). In every case it is not the absence of relation but the mystery of relation which is evoked. We have both light and darkness. Thus, Molloy's wholly unattractive mother attracts. For her he suffers. In her room he ends his days. He "must resemble her more and more." We are given keys that fail to unlock.

98

The diabolical method by which Beckett imitated the mysteries of relation in the overall form of his book was to divide it into two parts. The strategy is doubtless a result, in part, of Beckett's growing fascination with the possibilities of symmetrical composition which we observed in *Mercier et Camier*. Yet the division of *Molloy* is far less playful and gratuitous, far more disturbing, than the quadripartite division of the earlier work. It is effected in such a way that the reader's experience is that of reading two books masquerading as one. In *Mercier et Camier* the division functions as a container, abstract and inviolable. In *Molloy* it functions as an inseparable part of an imitation of life, generating in the reader much the same kind of experience that is generated in the narrators by their world.

The problem for the reader is that *Molloy* is divided into two parts that appear at once to be intimately related and to have no relation. The parts are distinct, yet they abound in parallels and cross-references. Essentially, this is a concentrated example of what Beckett does throughout his entire canon when he has names and objects reappear from work to work. But in *Molloy* the repeated elements seize the reader's attention with greater urgency because now the separate narratives are squeezed between the same covers. What echoes there are take on great weight because they are the only clues we have—in our obsession with unity—to go on in finding the connection. The strain is increased by the very abundance of parallels. William Faulkner's novel *The Wild Palms* is essentially two narratives that alternate chapter by chapter. In Faulkner's novel however, the narratives are so different and the parallels so few the reader accepts the fact that he is reading two different stories that, at most, provide an effective contrast to each other. But Moran is seeking Molloy (or Mollose, he is not sure). This is enough to lodge the hook. The parallels in turn force their way on the reader's consciousness. Here are a few of them: [4]

99

Molloy	Moran
On a quest for his mother.	On a quest for Molloy.
Writing a report under orders.	On the quest and writing a report under orders from Youdi (and the voice).
Enters a forest.	Stays on the edge of a forest.
Assaults a charcoal-burner.	Murders a stranger.
Observes two strangers.	Meets two strangers.
Employs a bicycle which he would love to describe at length.	Employs a bicycle which he would love to describe at length.
Undergoes degeneration of various limbs and organs.	Undergoes degeneration of various limbs and organs.
Uses a crutch.	Uses crutches after his return.
Attempts to devise a mathematic order for the carrying and sucking of sucking stones.	Attempts to devise a mathematical order for the wearing of his shirt on journey home.
Accosted and questioned by hostile policeman.	Accosted and questioned by hostile farmer.
Collector of his pages has a great thirst.	Gaber has a great thirst.
Wears a hat tied by a string which breaks.	Wears a hat tied by a string which breaks.
Remembers vaguely having a son.	Has a son.
Testicles hang a bit too low.	Testicles hang a bit too low.

As we have noted, the binary structure of *Molloy* seems to be one stage in an ongoing experiment with two-part form, what Fletcher calls the "asymmetrical diptych." [5] *Waiting for Godot* has a second act with much more exact echoes; the routines of Didi and Gogo, the visits of Pozzo and Lucky and the Boy recur in their allotted places. But precisely because the parallels are so close in *Godot*, their effect is the opposite of those in *Molloy*, for attention is drawn to the variations: the leaves on the tree, the shorter duration, the blindness of Pozzo. The second act is an imperfect version of the first, somewhat like Vladimir's second rendition of the round he tries to sing. Another, and again different, experiment with the form is found in *Play*, which was first performed in 1963. The second act in this work (which cannot properly be called a second act for the play describes itself as "a play in one act") is an exact repetition of the play.

Certainly these experiments have more in common than their dual structure. But the experiment in *Godot*, at least, relates most to our awareness of time. We observe that the same characters live on into Act II. The tree buds and Pozzo goes blind. And though we are not sure whether a day, a week, a season, or a year has passed, we wonder about it. We are very much aware, in other words, that the author is doing something with our sense of time.

This is not to say that a sense of temporal mysteries is not aroused by *Molloy*'s partitioning as well. Does Moran's voyage occur after Molloy's as the order of parts would suggest? If so, how long after? Or does Part I succeed Part II, and is Moran a prefiguring of Molloy (if he does not in fact become Molloy)? Or do the two parts occur at the same time? Is Moran searching for Molloy while Molloy is still eluding his pursuers; is Moran sent back once another agent has found Molloy at the edge of the forest? Or, finally, is Part I simply a rewrite of Part II after it has been remembered for the hundredth time? [6]

Yet the distinctness of the two reports, the lack of elements that lend continuity to *Godot*, make the anxiety of relation in a sense spatial as well as temporal. It is the more general nature of this anxiety which I am trying to define: the experience of an intimacy between two *patterns* without knowledge of their connection. The reader's dilemma, in other words, is not merely what he experiences in the temporal mysteries of past and present or cause and effect. It is what he experiences in all the mysteries of duality. The parts remain in the same suspension as A and C. As Molloy dealt with his subject, so Beckett deals with his—in a way that directly attacks notions of organic wholeness in art. We experience not the fusion of opposites, but the disconnection of similitudes.

The major formal experiment in *Molloy* is Beckett's use of the report as a narrative device. Its control over our response is continually operative, it helps enlarge a variety of mysteries, and as we shall see in the next chapter, it prepares vitally for our response to *Malone Dies*. The device itself is something Beckett toyed with in *Watt* when he created Sam with his little notebook. The difference, of course, between Sam and Molloy is great, mainly because in *Molloy* the report is much more a variant of first person narration in which the person narrating is the primary source of interest. The device, then, springs more directly from the stories— "The Expelled," "The End," "The Calmative," and "Premier amour" (the last as yet untranslated)—which were composed in the fall of 1946 (at approximately the same time as *Mercier et Camier; Molloy* was begun in 1947), and constitute Beckett's first prolonged experiments in first person narrative.

Compared to the works of the trilogy, however, the stories come closer to being authentic. Our attention is focused more fully on what is told rather than on the telling and its cause. There are just brief moments in these stories when the reader's attention is suddenly diverted from the narrative to its origins. The narrator of "The Expelled," for example, finishes by confessing,

"I don't know why I told this story, I could just as well have told another," [7] and the narrator of "The End" concludes: "The memory came faint and cold of the story I might have told, a story in the likeness of my life, I mean without the courage to end or the strength to go on." [8] In "The Calmative" the narrator begins by telling us he is dead and because he is too frightened to listen to himself rot he will tell himself a story:

> I'll try and tell myself another story, to try and calm myself, and it's there I feel I'll be old, old, even older than the day I fell, calling for help, and it came. Or is it possible that in this story I have come back to life, after my death? No, it's not like me to come back to life, after my death.[9]

In the trilogy these points are, as it were, expanded so that the mysteries within the narrative are compounded far more by mysteries of and behind the narrative process. In *The Unnamable*, the narrative barely materializes at all. Perhaps this is what Beckett meant when, asked to compare his work with Kafka's, he said that in the latter "the consternation is is the form. In my work there is consternation behind the form." [10]

In this regard, the report, as a narrative device, was a stroke of genius. I imagine the inspiration was—as for so much else in *Molloy*—the popular mystery or tale of espionage. It is "The Statement of Sergeant Cuff's Man" expanded to the point where it takes up the entire book. Accompanying the report is the suggestion of an elaborate bureaucracy—too hopelessly involved and secretive to allow any mortal a glimpse of its final cause. Here, at least, the effect is certainly reminiscent of Kafka, a commentary on the profound inadequacy of human comprehension. It is as if to say that when confronted with metaphysical mysteries the mind can produce only the models of bureaucracy. Thus when the mind becomes aware of an urge or need, it strives to define what it feels in terms of bureaucratic structure: Who is making commands? For what ends? By what agent? Responsible to whom? Employing what sanctions?

Now it is in the nature of reports that they require a specific purpose in order that they be justified. Report for what? A novel, however, escapes this condition inasmuch as it is assumed that novels are written for those who read novels. Whether or not the novel reader can define his reasons for reading novels, the novelist is happy to satisfy the basic appetite. But by composing fiction in the form of a report, Beckett reminds us of the problem of ends. Sergeant Cuff's man made his statement for Sergeant Cuff, and with its aid Sergeant Cuff solved a mystery. But Molloy writes his pages for he does not know whom or what. He is paid by the page, "Yet I don't work for money. For what then? I don't know" (p. 7). Handled in this way, the form generates at once the contradictory feelings of urgency and gratuitousness. It recalls in part the conception of art Beckett developed in the Duthuit dialogues: "The expression that there is . . . no desire to express, together with the obligation to express." [11]

Moran, in his turn, is ordered to write for Youdi. But who is Youdi? And what need has he of the report? Youdi and Gaber, by adding "light" (in contrast to the sparser indications of authority in Molloy's section), extend this mystery. For determining the value of the report is contingent upon determining the nature or at least value of the bureaucracy that contains it. Yet all we know of the bureaucracy, what light we have, we get from the report. And the report, being merely a report, fails to evaluate that from which its value is derived. A novel, in contrast, is generally charged with responsibility in two areas: the descriptive and the normative. The novelist is expected to instruct and interpret while being faithful to actuality. A report—the kind of descriptive report that Molloy and Moran are charged with—is relieved of this dual obligation. Its pretensions are only to fact. Interpretation, comment, and instruction must be left to the proper authorities ("Gaber, he said, life is a thing of beauty, Gaber, and a joy for ever" [p. 164]). And yet we, too, have the report—at least it has fallen into our hands. We have these data, and data cry to be interpreted. Reports are for something; they are not to be wasted. But how can we begin? Youdi is not available for comment, and the authors' obligations end with fact.

But the concern for fact, in its turn, introduces a host of new problems. The expectations of fact, which a report automatically arouses, amplify the effect of Beckett's characteristically decrepit narrators. So that just as, in the way we discussed above, the report augments anxiety about issues of evaluation if not metaphysics, so by its very pretensions to fact it augments anxiety about issues of epistemology. A report may very well pretend to fact, "but to tell the truth (to tell the truth!)," as Molloy says, is another matter. Can we hope to know what happened? To begin with, there is the problem of composition: "I always say either too much or too little, which is a terrible thing for a man with a passion for truth like mine" (p. 34). Molloy (and Moran in the later stages of his report) often reminds us of the awesome gap that falls between the world and the words that pretend to be about the world ("To restore silence is the role of objects" [p. 13]). Molloy's report fills up into one black paragraphless block of words—which serves also to remind us that the report is, before it is anything else, words.

To go on, there is the next gap—that between the mind and the world. It is the problem of the senses. How accurate was the recording device at the time of the recorded events? Beckett's tool here is the sadly decaying vision of his reporters. The effect achieved is similar to the tunnel vision and flicker of early film. Objects and figures often appear with brilliant clarity, but the scene rarely accompanies them. The narrative is a sequence of points of focus without context. In addition, there is the flicker. Things appear and disappear with disconcerting abruptness: "then he began to straighten the tables and chairs I had overturned and to put them back into place, dusting them as he did so with a feather duster which suddenly appeared in his hand" (p. 43).

These are two initial problems: composing and seeing. Compound them and the result is passages like this:

> The room was dark and full of people hastening to and fro, malefactors, policemen, lawyers, priests, and journalists, I suppose. All that made a dark, dark forms crowding in a dark place. They paid no attention to me and I repaid the compliment. Then how could I know they were paying no attention to me, and how could I repay the compliment, since they were paying no attention to me? I don't know. I knew it and I did it, that's all I know. But suddenly a woman rose up before me. . . [P. 23]

But if these problems were not problems—if the eyes were fixed and the vocabulary expanded—would the task necessarily be simpler or the results better? Note Molloy's ambiguity when he comments on his seashore experiences: "And not only did I see more clearly, but I had less difficulty in saddling with a name the rare things I saw. These are some of the advantages and disadvantages of the seaside" (p. 75). For if we saw more clearly, we would be saddled with more to name. And if we could saddle things more easily with names, would they necessarily be the right names? "If I go on long enough calling that my life, I'll end up by believing it. It's the principle of advertising" (p. 53). And whether they are wrong or right, names in Beckett always carry with them the possible disadvantage (and advantage) of exorcising the things they name.

There remains the gap between past and present: a gap greatly increased by the decrepitude of our narrator's memory. In this gap lies imagination. The theme is articulated in Molloy's description of C. It is a gentle parody but, nevertheless, as much Beckett as Wordsworth: "But now he knows these hills, that is to say he knows them better, and if ever again he sees them from afar it will be I think with other eyes, and not only that but the within, all that inner space one never sees, the brain and heart and other caverns where thought and feeling dance their sabbath, all that too quite differently disposed" (p. 10). To call it a gap is a bit misleading. It implies that the reporter must only reconcile two images —the original and the present—while in fact the image is in a constant flux of re-creation through the dance of thought and feeling "Yes, it was an orange pomeranian, the less I think of it the more certain I am" (p. 12).

This variety of inexactitude brings us at last to our sense of the relationship that exists between our reporters and their reports—a mystery that in a sense contains all others. It is imitated in form most directly through two stylistic innovations that our narrators, Molloy particularly, introduce into their reports. The first is what Molloy calls the "mythological present": "I speak in the present tense, it is so easy to speak in the present tense, when speaking of the past. It is the mythological present, don't mind it" (p. 26). The result is passages like these:

> I will not tell what followed, for I am weary of this place, I want to go. It was late afternoon when they told me I could go. [P. 24]

> But now I shall have to get myself out of this ditch. How joyfully I would vanish there, sinking deeper

and deeper under the rains. No doubt I'll come back some day, here, or to a similar slough. [P. 27]

The house where Lousse lived. Must I describe it? I don't think so. I won't, that's all I know, for the moment. Perhaps later on, if I get to know it. And Lousse? Must I describe her? I suppose so. Let's first bury the dog. [P. 35]

The second innovation is a variant of the mythological present which might be termed "creative reportage" and gives rise to passages like these:

I got to my knees, no, that doesn't work, I got up and watched the little procession recede. [P. 19]

Then, nicely balanced on my crutches, I began to swing, backwards, forwards, feet pressed together, or rather legs pressed together, for how could I press my feet together, with my legs in the state they were? But how could I press my legs together, in the state they were? I pressed them together, that's all I can tell you. Take it or leave it. Or I didn't press them together. What can that possibly matter? I swung, that's all that matters . . . [P. 84]

Then I went back into the house and wrote, It is midnight. The rain is beating on the windows. It was not midnight. It was not raining. [P. 176]

The combined effect of these stylistic departures is to suggest that the exercise of reporting the past is at once creative and experiential: "For in describing this day I am once more he who suffered it, who crammed it full of futile anxious life. . . . And as then my thoughts would have none of Molloy, so tonight my pen" (p. 122). In consequence our two reporters are changing as much in the journey of composition as they did in the original journey they write of, and this change in turn affects both what and how they write. Thus Moran, transformed at the end of a journey in prose, which followed some earlier journey on foot, can return to where he began eighty-five pages ago and with his new vision push off once again on a revised version of the same old journey: "It was not midnight. It was not raining."

The process is more dramatic in Moran because he has a longer way to go. One may observe it in the change of style and tone which, as Ruby Cohn has noted, gradually occurs during the composition of his report.[12] One may also observe it in the growing urgency and clarity of Moran's internal voice, which in the early stages of composition he is "only just beginning to know" (p. 132), but which by the end is coming in strong. And one may again observe it in Moran's increasing certainty, as he composes, that in the future he will have to leave again on another journey: an idea that at first horrifies him ("I am too old to lose all this, and begin again, I am too old!" [p. 132]) but he grows to accept, so that by the end he is simply "clearing out."

Thus what masquerades as two reports is actually two original compositions, compositions that in turn effect their creators as actual experiences. Reporting, in short, is not a matter of recollecting in tranquillity but a matter of creating and undergoing. Molloy and Moran, seeking to report the facts of their experience, to define themselves, tell a series of lies, or stories, which in turn become facts of their experience—facts that in turn can never be reported except through a new series of lies. One has a vision of endless cycles, as does Beckett's next narrator, Malone. But Malone is much too cagey to follow willingly the route of his immediate predecessors. And Beckett, having exhausted the imitative potential of the report, was to help him out by giving an initial push in another direction.

6

An Exercise-Book

IN GENERAL readers of the trilogy have tended to view it as a kind of linear continuum that starts at one point and advances by a direct line of descent to another point. In developing this view, the only problem that has caused any serious difficulty is that of finessing Moran's narrative so that it is seen somehow to precede Molloy's. As for the second book of the trilogy, it is usually assumed that it stands midway on this path—that, in terms of the spatial metaphor, it begins at a point below *Molloy* and leads downward to *The Unnamable*. The view is certainly encouraged by a few salient features of *Malone Dies*, particularly the narrator's physical condition which represents a distinct advance over his predecessors and, as it concludes in death, prepares logically for the disembodied voice that takes up in *The Unnamable*. The same can be said of Malone's isolation. Unlike his predecessors, he has no notion whose room he inhabits. He has no Gaber to bring him messages. His maid deserts him. He loses control of his possessions. And his speech and hearing fail. Furthermore, what I referred to in the last chapter as the mystery behind the narrative is augmented in *Malone Dies* by having proportionately more of the book devoted to the narrator's "present state." Again, this would seem to be part of a linear descent to *The Unnamable*, a book that is entirely "present state."

There is certainly no disputing that Beckett tried to develop a progression here, a "descent" as we have been calling it. Nevertheless, to generalize from these elements to *Malone Dies* as a whole, or to let our interpretation of the book be dominated by this sense of progression, is a mistake. There is too much in *Malone Dies* which resists the attempt—much, indeed, which gives the book more the appearance of a departure than a continuation. Malone, to begin with, is not under orders, a fact that immediately distinguishes him from Molloy, Moran, and the speaker of *The Unnamable*. We have no references to a voice, external or internal, which drives him to compose. On the contrary, we have a willful old gentleman who undertakes to play a game. Moreover, being an omniscient storyteller and in addition one who improves (Macmann's, I think, is a better, or at least more interesting story than Sapo's), he is endowed with a certain ability to create. Needless to say, he is somewhat less than a master, and more than one of his projects come to grief. Yet the main project Malone sets himself—"to show myself . . . on the point of vanishing, at the same time as the stranger" (p. 195)—does appear, as author and tale fade out together, to have been pulled off. It is a neat trick, or as he puts it, "no ordinary last straw."

One speaks in comparative terms, of course. Yet there is no denying that Malone's (comparative) independence, his storytelling, his determination to play, and his (somewhat qualified) success are unique in the context of the trilogy. They give the book, as I say, more the aspect of a respite or digression than a continuation. In short, *Malone Dies* seems at once to be leading toward and leading away from *The Unnamable*.

The cause of this can be made clear I think by comparing a passage in the English *Molloy* with its French original: "This time, then once more I think, then perhaps a last time, then I think it'll be over, with that world too. Premonition of the last but one but one" (p. 8). Thus in English Molloy forecasts the trilogy. But in the French version he says, "Cette fois-ci, puis encore une je pense, puis c'en sera fini je pense, de ce monde-là aussi. C'est le sens de l'avant-dernier," [1] forecasting only one more attempt. Fletcher estimates from this that when Beckett began writing *Molloy, The Unnamable* was as yet unforeseen.[2] I think he is right. It is a point that deserves emphasis, for what it implies is that Beckett started with a unit of two books in mind, not three: companion pieces that ended logically with the death of the narrator. Only later as *The Unnamable* grew in his mind did the idea of a trilogy, and with it the idea of a descending progression, develop.

Seeing these first two books as companion pieces, facing each other as it were, rather than leading somewhere, helps explain several things. The seeming inversion of the two parts of *Molloy,* for example, becomes somewhat less problematic if only by our understanding that *Molloy* was not originally planned as part of an implacable march to the depths. It also helps account for the comparatively great distance between *Malone Dies* and *The Unnamable,* for *Molloy* and *Malone Dies,* being companion pieces, are developed on the same plane. They share the same order of narrative and imagistic coherence. In *The Unnamable,* however, we suddenly take a giant step downward into a radically different kind of fiction in which narrative and imagistic coherence of any kind is eliminated.

One could almost say that it is *Molloy* and not *Malone Dies* which leads to *The Unnamable.* The report, that is, shaping itself more and more to the flux and uncertainty of its subject, becomes finally the subject itself. The last four sentences of *Molloy* show where it is going; they are in fact a fine anticipation of the last sentence of *The Unnamable.* With stories, however, we are given a reprieve. For, though they too are required to imitate life, they are also allowed, indeed required, to give it form and so depart from life. They have a license the report lacks. It is this feature of stories that attracts Malone. He serves clear notice at the outset

112

that the concern for fact that troubled the reporters of *Molloy*—"my old quibbles" as he calls it—is a cross he now refuses to bear. "That is the kind of bait I do not rise to anymore, my need for prettiness is gone" (p. 179). "Now," he says, "it's a game, I am going to play" (p. 180). He has tried this before but has always failed because within him "the wild beast of earnestness padded up and down, roaring, ravening, rending" (p. 194). It was Molloy's "passion for truth" that spoiled the fun. It made him rise to the bait for worrying about accuracy. But the way out is now at hand, and it lies in stories. As Molloy recognized long before while still trapped in his report: "What I need now is stories, it took me a long time to know that" (p. 13).

As far as Malone is concerned, then, his enterprise is an attempt to avoid the misery of his forebears. He is going to find a way of coexisting with his ignorance, and he is going to find a way of coexisting with himself. There is an old weak joke that catches something of the quality of his method: if we had any ham, we could make some ham and eggs, if we had any eggs. The quality is that of a world in apodosis. "I could die today," he writes, "if I wished, merely by making a little effort, if I could wish, if I could make an effort" (p. 179). He tries, then, to fill his exercise-book with a variety of possibilities—essentially exercises—in the absence of terms, evidence, and, hopefully, Malone. The story is the world in apodosis. One admits the absence of terms, surety, knowledge, and goes right ahead building a world. In the absence of ham, in the absence of eggs, one can still make a kind of ham and eggs.

The question then arises, if Malone is trying to play or escape, why should he produce, of all things, the adventures of Sapo and Macmann? Why, in other words, should he build a world that so strikingly resembles all the previous mess of the canon? For surely Malone, of all Beckett's protagonists, could escape this. As we noted, he is unique in not being under orders. There is neither voice nor master, just a frosty old gentleman who, it would appear, has been granted the freedom to be perfectly arbitrary. Yet we pass through the looking glass in *Malone Dies* and return to the world we thought we left. Having descended by stages from the omniscient perspective of *Murphy* to the peculiar inside and outside perspective of *Watt* and then to the intimate first person reportage of *Molloy*, we pass in this book to the eye of the creator himself. But we go right on through the eye to find on the other side projects of omniscience involving a man and a woman and a boy. And reflected in these we see, in effect, the whole past canon stretching out ahead of us.

The answer to our question, obviously, is that Malone cannot escape and that his book is a demonstration of this. Furthermore, by so demonstrating, *Malone Dies* becomes a mirror to its companion, *Molloy*. This, I believe, was Beckett's original intention when he conceived of a plan involving two books. We have essentially the same "mess" in both works, but approached from opposite directions. In *Molloy* Beckett employed reportage and a direct concern with fact and self; in *Malone Dies* he employed Malone's desire to tell stories, to play, and to escape. The mirror effect that results can be summed up in this way: where in *Molloy*, as we saw in the last chapter, reportage becomes creation, in *Malone Dies* creation becomes reportage. To elaborate, in *Molloy* we have two narrators under strict orders to report a certain passage from each of their lives and who, in the process of reporting, become involved in the process of creating, of lying, of making up stories about themselves; in *Malone Dies* we have one narrator under no orders but those of his fancy who, in the process of making up stories, becomes involved in the process of reporting, that is, of telling stories very much in the image of what we imagine to have been his life. Thus *Molloy* depicts the impossibility of defining one's self, while *Malone Dies* depicts the impossibility of escaping one's self. "I wonder if I am not talking yet again about myself," Malone asks, "Shall I be incapable, to the end, of lying on any other subject?" (p. 189). His complaint defines a midpoint between freedom and certainty to which all three narrators are doomed. They are all constrained to a lifetime of lying on the same subject.

It would be unfair, however, to the complexity of *Malone Dies* to leave its hero's objectives as we have defined them. That he creates his own "mortal tedium" in the very stories he writes to escape it is a fact he recognizes almost immediately. It is only in rare moments that he is able to convince himself that he is "elsewhere," far from himself, observing the sufferings of a stranger. "I have only to open my mouth for it to testify to the old story, my old story" (p. 236). But Malone is subtle. And having conceived his plan and almost at the same time foreseen its sad conclusion, he begins to graft onto it new objectives. Some of these simply have the effect of pointing up the absurdity of his enterprise, for example: "It is right that he [Sapo] too should have his little chronicle, his memories, his reason, and be able to recognize the good in the bad, the bad in the worst . . . that is my excuse. But there must be others, no less excellent" (p. 208). He does formulate one objective, however, that I think is far more clever than any of the others. It is intriguing because it is a kind of ultimate compromise. The plan, presented like the others with hesitation, doubt, and denial, is this: "to try and live, cause to live, be another, in myself, in another" (p. 195). It is a possible way of converting his failure into an achievement, that is, of turning the distressing similarity between his creatures and himself into something positive. In trying to "be another, in myself, in another," he makes his stories not simply an attempt to escape himself but an attempt at the same time to define himself. It is, to repeat, an ultimate compromise. In play he will create another, and so appease his craving to leave himself. And yet by creat-

115

ing another he will provide a vehicle for his self, the old earnestness, and so appease the other craving. "Yes, a little creature, I shall try and make a little creature, to hold in my arms, a little creature in my image, no matter what I say" (p. 226). It makes his stories a prelude to the frenzied hide-and-seek the next narrator will play with his creatures, Mahood and Worm. Furthermore, Malone sees, long before his successor, the plan's inevitable failure: "Yes, a little creature. . . . And seeing what a poor thing I have made, or how like myself, I shall eat it. Then be alone a long time, unhappy, not knowing what my prayer should be nor to whom" (p. 226).

The key formal strategy Beckett used to express his subject is that of simply alternating Malone's stories with his "present state." Thus the experience that gives Malone so much trouble becomes part of our experience as we pass from one to the other. The device allowed Beckett to develop an interchange in which qualities of the present state recur in the stories, and qualities of the stories recur in the present state. Thus, as we have already had occasion to note, Sapo and Macmann, in their decrepitude and incompetence, are re-creations of Malone. Indeed, everywhere Malone turns in his storytelling he comes upon himself, so that even when he happens to digress or to describe some incidental scene, what results is still infused with aspects of his present state. You will recall, for example, that when Malone rediscovers Sapo, now Macmann, he pauses to give a somewhat rambling description of the homeward journeys of townsfolk after work (229–231). The crowd he describes is composed for the most part of "solitaries pressing forward through the throng," hastening toward home in the growing dusk. "And God help him," Malone notes, "who longs, for once, in his recovered freedom, to walk a little way with a fellow-creature." He who rides in a cab through "the press of misplaced persons" travels in "the dark box that encloses him." The cabman rides "all alone on his box." "And each one has his reasons, while wondering from time to time what they are worth, and if they are the true ones, for going where he is going, rather than somewhere else, and the horse hardly less darkly than the men." What we have, in short, is the darkness and isolation of the author re-created in the scene.

Consider another aspect of Malone's present state: his nearly complete helplessness, his inability to control what goes on around him. He depends on a maid who deserts him and a stick that he loses. A man dressed in black suddenly raps on his skull, sits staring at him for twelve hours and departs. There is as little controlling as there is accounting for it. His precious possessions, the things of all the world most intimate with him, are beyond his grasp once he loses his stick. And even when he can still move them about, he is troubled by their obstinate refusal to remain the same. He discovers things he cannot remember having and loses things he cannot remember losing. Thus, "knowing perfectly well" he had no exercise-book, he can nonetheless pull one out of his possessions: "if tomorrow I needed an old love-letter I would adopt the same method" (p. 209). In addition to the "changing aspect" of his possessions, his room, too, changes. The walls and floor grow whiter (p. 223). The window becomes rounder (p. 237). Even the world beyond is no more dependable than the rest:

Example, there is nothing like examples, I was once in utter darkness and waiting with some impatience for dawn to break, having need of its light to see to certain little things which it is difficult to see to in the dark. And sure enough little by little the dark lightened and I was able to hook with my stick the objects I required. But the light, instead of being the dawn, turned out in a very short time to be the dusk. And the sun, instead of rising higher and higher in the sky as I confidently expected, calmly set, and night, the passing of which I had just celebrated after my fashion, calmly fell again. [P. 220]

Now stories, one might guess, would at least offer an escape from this aspect of Malone's present state. As a storyteller, he is given a chance to select his material and manipulate it according to his will. Yet almost immediately Malone finds himself toiling with material that refuses to submit. His befuddlement here can be equally funny:

> The first time an exasperated master threatened him with a cane, Sapo snatched it from his hand and threw it out of the window, which was closed, for it was winter. This was enough to justify his expulsion. But Sapo was not expelled, either then or later. I must try and discover, when I have time to think about it quietly, why Sapo was not expelled, when he so richly deserved to be. For I want as little as possible of darkness in his story. A little darkness, in itself, at the time, is nothing. You think no more about it and you go on. But I know what darkness is, it accumulates, thickens, then suddenly bursts and drowns everything.
>
> I have not been able to find out why Sapo was not expelled. I shall have to leave this question open. I try not to be glad. I shall make haste to put a safe remove between him and this incomprehensible indulgence. I shall make him live as though he had been punished according to his deserts. We shall turn our backs on this little cloud, but we shall not let it out of our sight. It will not cover the sky without our knowing, we shall not suddenly raise our eyes, far from help, far from shelter, to a sky as black as ink. That is what

I have decided. I see no other solution. It is the best I can do. [P. 190]

His stories thus appear to have a life beyond that endowed them by their creator. He loses Sapo as he lost his boot. And when he finds him again, Sapo is completely transformed by events he knows nothing of: "I have taken a long time to find him. How did I know it was he, I don't know. . . . And what can have changed him so? Life perhaps, the struggle to love, to eat, to escape the redressors of wrongs. . . . I ran him down in the heart of the town, sitting on a bench. How did I know it was he? The eyes perhaps. No, I don't know how I knew, I'll take back nothing. Perhaps it is not he" (p. 226). The changing aspect of his possessions is repeated in the changing aspect of his creatures. And his game with stories appears more often than not an attempt to report the truth about some actuality he dimly apprehends. And so, a day later, when Macmann reappears in the House of Saint John of God, Malone is not at all sure if it is the same Macmann, born Sapo, whom he discovered in the park. For after all, "the Macmanns are legion in the island and pride themselves, what is more, with few exceptions, on having one and all, in the last analysis, sprung from the same illustrious ball. It is therefore inevitable they should resemble one another, now and then, to the point of being confused even in the minds of those who wish them well and would like nothing better than to tell between them" (p. 259).

Thus Malone returns to his "old quibbles." Not only do his stories bear his image, but he relates to them in much the same way he relates to his present state: with mystification and loss of control. But Malone is on the alert for this. He is, after all, telling stories now. There should be no need for the elaborate hypotheses and computations of his predecessors. So he makes valiant efforts to thwart his "need for prettiness." The result is a parody of the fictionist's license. His narrative is riddled with improvisations:

> Then Lemuel took it from him and struck him with it over and over again, no, that won't work, then Lemuel called a keeper by the name of Pat . . . [P. 275]

> Monday the feet, Tuesday the legs up to the knees, Wednesday the thighs, and so on, culminating on Sunday with the neck and ears, no, Sunday he rested from washing. [P. 257]

The more his material resists him, the more he abuses his license. Particularly as he approaches his death and therefore, according to his plan, what is supposed to be the conclusion of his narrative, he becomes increasingly reckless, his humor cut more and more by desperation. Is it really Macmann, his Macmann, he finds in the House of Saint John of God? "No matter," he says, "any old remains of flesh and spirit do, there is no sense in stalking people. So long as it is what is called a living being you can't go wrong, you have the guilty one" (p. 259). In the last stages of his narrative, he finds to his chagrin that his story has proliferated a host of creatures who, for some reason, stand in the way of his denouement. His only recourse is to begin murdering them. "Moll," he says, "I'm going to kill her." This accomplished and still no end in sight, Lemuel is set to work, hacking and butchering. But even Lemuel is not up to the task, so that in the end Malone is left with only one alternative, which he manages in his last breath:

> never anything

> there

> any more

120

As I have suggested, such free manipulation is one of the advantages Malone seeks in stories. Yet it is a phenomenon by no means restricted to his "fictional" material. For if we cross back now to the present state, we find that it too is riddled with the same kind of arbitrary adjustments that Malone makes so often in his stories:

> When my chamber-pot is full I put it on the table, beside the dish. Then I go twenty-four hours without a pot. No, I have two pots. They have thought of everything. [P. 185]

> I drew a line, no, I did not even draw a line, and I wrote, soon I shall be quite dead at last, and so on. [P. 209]

And these adjustments are nothing compared to the gradual evolution of Malone's portrait of himself. It is a transformation one is likely to overlook, absorbed as one is in the increasingly violent and erratic nature of the stories. Yet if one reads through the passages of present state, one will notice immediately how astonishing and dramatic this process is: much more extreme, I think, than anything that occurs in the stories. In effect, Malone evolves from a literal old man to a protean and mythic fantasy.

One starts with an old man in bed. He tells us that he has a "big shaggy head." He ventures to say of his ears that they are embellished by "two impetuous tufts of no doubt yellow hair, yellowed by wax and lack of care, and so long that the lobes are hidden" (p. 207). He garnishes the facts, perhaps, but remains within or near the realm of empirical probability. "I have demanded certain movements of my legs and even feet. I know them well and could feel the effort they made to obey. I have lived with them that little space of time, filled with drama, between the message received and the piteous response" (p. 191). But as his body dies, Malone's description of himself becomes increasingly metaphorical. The old man on the bed is gradually replaced by a succession of fantastic improvisations. "The sensation is familiar of a blind and tired hand delving feebly in my particles and letting them trickle between its fingers. And sometimes, when all is quiet, I feel it plunged in me up to the elbow, but gentle, and as though sleeping. But soon it stirs, wakes, fondles, clutches, ransacks, ravages, avenging its failure to scatter me with one sweep" (p. 224). There are "the times when I go liquid and become like mud," and the times "when I would be lost in the eye of a needle, I am so hard and contracted" (p. 225). He is "an old foetus" who will "land head foremost mewling in the charnelhouse" (p. 225). Yet, "if I were to stand up again, from which God preserve me, I fancy I would fill a considerable part of the universe" (p. 235). As for his feet, they are "leagues away. And to call them in, to be cleaned for example, would I think take me over a month, exclusive of the time required to locate them. . . . I feel they are beyond the range of the most powerful telescope" (p. 234). Moreover, "if my arse suddenly started to shit at the present moment, which God forbid, I firmly believe the lumps would fall out in Australia" (p. 235).

Observe, too, how his room is subjected to the same process. Thus, what began as "just a plain private room apparently, in what appears to be a plain ordinary house" (p. 183), becomes a series of extraordinary hypotheses: "a kind of vault" surrounded by "a wide trench or ditch with other vaults opening upon it" (p. 219) or "a head and . . . these eight, no, six, these six planes that enclose me are of solid bone" (p. 221). "A kind of air circulates"; he does not know if it is "the kind that lends itself to the comedy of combustion," but "when all goes still I can hear it beating against the walls" (p.

221). When at last he takes his leave of the reader, room and creature combine in a final violent collage:

> I am swelling. What if I should burst? The ceiling rises and falls, rises and falls, rhythmically, as when I was a foetus. Also to be mentioned a noise of rushing water, phenomenon mutatis mutandis perhaps analogous to that of the mirage, in the desert. . . . Leaden light again, thick, eddying, riddled with little tunnels through to brightness, perhaps I should say air, sucking air. All is ready. Except me. I am being given, if I may venture the expression, birth to into death, such is my impression. The feet are clear already, of the great cunt of existence. Favorable presentation I trust. My head will be the last to die. Haul in your hands. I can't. The render rent. My story ended I'll be living yet. Promising lag. That is the end of me. I shall say I no more. [P. 283]

Thus Malone the reporter exercises certainly as much creative improvisation in describing his present state as does Malone the creator exercise in composing his stories. Death in Malone's case is simply an end to metaphor. For reporting the self is a doomed and potentially infinite literary experiment, just as telling stories is a continual return to the self. Nowhere in Beckett's canon, I think, does he define with such dense compression this paradoxical combination. The key was merely the expedient formal device of alternating stories with present state. As is so often the case with Beckett, it is dazzling in its simplicity.

7

Text

"BUT LET US leave these morbid matters and get on with that of my demise. . . . Then it will be all over with these Murphys, Merciers, Morans and Malones, unless it goes on beyond the grave" (p. 236). I am sure one should not take the implications of Malone's afterthought too literally. To place the last book of the trilogy in the life beyond would be to mitigate Beckett's skepticism considerably. Yet so different is *The Unnamable* from its predecessors that it does appear to represent a kind of fictional afterlife. It is, in a sense, the way the author has of carrying on after the death of fiction. I say "in a sense" meaning in the absence of two essential aspects of fiction: some appearance of beginning and ending and the presence of visual imagery. All one can really count on in *The Unnamable* is varieties of words and syntax.

In 1950, shortly after Beckett completed *The Unnamable,* he composed *Texts for Nothing.* I would guess that many of the texts originated as rough sketches for *The Unnamable.* I have no way of proving this, and certainly there are differences between the two books which have on occasion been noted: the humor, present still on every page, but darker in the texts; new motifs such as the courtroom conceit of text 5 and certain oblique harbingers of *How It Is;* and the separation into thirteen units—an experiment that could perhaps have led to the rapid pulsation of page and print in *How It Is.* As Cohn suggests, too, "the quest of the 'I'" appears to be "even more single-minded and compulsively absurd than that of *The Unnamable*." [1] But formally, I think, Beckett attempted essentially the same thing in these "words without acts" [2] as he did in *The Unnamable*.

The main reason I bring them up here at the beginning is because of their curious title. Fletcher provides this note: "the title of the thirteen Texts for Nothing is based on the musical term *mesure pour rien,* meaning 'a bar's rest.' Thus a *texte pour rien* would be a grouping of words conveying nothing, and this is in fact, more or less, what we find." [3] This would seem likely, especially as the texts reveal other "musical" characteristics that Fletcher goes on to point out. The analogy with music, however, does present one problem if we are going to interpret these texts as a "grouping of words conveying nothing": that is, in music a *mesure pour rien* is far from being without musical meaning. It has, in fact, as much meaning as a measure composed of notes. It cannot even be called silence. But perhaps this is an irony that the author had in mind when he titled his work. For, surely, his narrators are as far from achieving certainty of nothing as they are of something.

The term I find most interesting is "text." It is true that one meaning of "text" is the words for a song, which would coincide with the musical idea Fletcher toys with. This is oblique, however, and I think it unlikely that Beckett had it in mind. Yet when one surveys the standard definitions (*Oxford English Dictionary*) of "text," one finds that the word, at least formally, describes almost nothing at all:

1. the wording of anything written,
2. the very wording of anything written,
3. the very wording of Scripture.

One is left with "wording" that in context, of course, is redundant. Beckett would have done just as well to have entitled his work *For Nothing*. By including "texts" in the title, he achieves an ultimate modesty in which the only pretension to artistic form is words, period.

"Text" can also mean the short passage from the Scriptures so often employed as a subject for sermons. Figuratively, as the *OED* phrases it, this becomes "the theme or subject on which anyone speaks; the starting point of a discussion; a statement on which anyone dilates." This is certainly apt, and Beckett may have had it in mind. By this definition Beckett's texts are passages or fragments from a whole, though in this case the whole is never known. They are also starting points, the text being that on which discussion develops. As is obvious, the discussion never really gets going and the texts remain texts.

What I wish to emphasize is the bareness of this term as a formal description. With *The Unnamable* and *Texts*, Beckett has at last produced fiction—if one still wishes to call it that—which is sheer text. A common, and certainly creditable, way to account for this is to view these two works as part of an organic sequence: a process of formal corruption which, as I suggested in the chapter on *Mercier et Camier*, the author has both encouraged and fought throughout his career. Thus the death of Malone marks the death of a certain literary experiment, and in *The Unnamable* Beckett tries to resuscitate what is left of the corpse.

Beckett, however, is not as wholly at the mercy of this process as on occasion he has led us to believe. As I argued in the last chapter, it is pretty clear that the notion of a sequential decline in the trilogy was a formal idea that Beckett "added" to his companion pieces once the original project was underway. What I am suggesting is that the helpless author helps himself so that it is possible to look in turn at *The Unnamable* as another separate project—this time involving a severe limitation of subject, which in turn requires certain formal adjustments. Beckett narrows his focus in *The Unnamable* to the speaker's search for a self behind the self, that which pushes the words, for which as yet neither story nor image exists. It is announced in the very first words— "Where now? Who now? When now?"—the unknown self wedged in unknown space and time.[4] This is not to say that the questions of who and what they were did not plague Beckett's other creatures. But the subject of the other works was broader, less exclusively focused on this search for the interior self. The elements of human contact, for example, and love were properly part of the earlier fiction because they were part of the broader subject it struggled to accommodate.

The formal decay is most apparent in the disappearance of two major adjuncts of fiction. These are story, or at least something with recognizable beginning and ending, and place, or at least some sense of secure visual imagery: in short, time and space. Considering the change of focus, the necessity of this decay is perfectly logical. If our subject is a self that lies outside our notions of time and space then it follows, according to the theory of imitative form, that a major formal objective will be the obliteration of these notions insofar as they inhere in form.

Thus, to begin with its temporal qualities, *The Unnamable*, except for the start and finish of its print, truly has no recognizable beginning or end. It is not properly a "work" at all but rather a segment of process: a constant grinding out of new beginnings from old endings with a countermotion that chews up the new beginnings as they appear. "Let us first suppose, in order to get on a little, then we'll suppose something else, in order to get on a little further, that it is in fact required of me that I say something, something that is not to be found in all I have said up to now. That seems a reasonable assumption. But thence to infer that the something required is something about me suddenly strikes me as unwarranted" (p. 311). There is no grand finale in sight, not even a demise as in the case of Malone. There are only beginnings, exordia, preambles, undertaken in the hope that they shall lead the speaker to himself. The hope he constantly repeats is that "this preamble will soon come to an end and the statement begin that will dispose of me" (p. 302). Yet at the "end" of the book he is beginning again: "you must go on, I can't go on, I'll go on." And even if a cessation were accomplished, what significance could be attributed to it? "I was grievously mistaken," he says, "in supposing that death in itself could be regarded as evidence, or even a strong presumption, in support of a preliminary life" (p. 342). It is a lesson, perhaps, learned from Malone. Death is too inconclusive. And so, unlike Malone, the speaker has "no longer the least desire to leave this world, in which they keep trying to foist me, without some kind of assurance that I was really there, such as a kick in the arse, for example, or a kiss" (p. 342).

The spatial, or visual, aspect of the work is equally unsettling. Gone is all sense of place, all rooms, all limbs, specificity as to the number of toes, possessions, creations. Mahood, who briefly lightens the pages—first in a Ulyssean trek, then in a jar—is a fiasco that is swept away with the rest of the canon. Worm is simply a name, the promise of more without the substance that bobs in a sea of prose. As the speaker says, "it is solely a question of voices, no other image is appropriate" (p. 347). The other members of the canon, the speaker's "delegates" who put in appearances for him elsewhere, are all brought to judgment at the outset and fired: "All these Murphys, Molloys and Malones do not fool me. They have made me waste my time, suffer for nothing, speak of them when, in order to stop speaking, I should have spoken of me and me alone" (p. 303). They have concerned themselves with "things that don't concern me, that don't count, that I don't believe, that they have crammed me full of to prevent me from saying who I am, and from doing what I have to do in the only way that can put an end to it, from doing what I have to do. How they must hate me!" (p. 324). The experiments with Mahood are a fiasco because they are a lapse, a falling into the habits of his predecessors. "Help, help," he cries, "if I could only describe this place, I who am so good at describing places, walls, ceilings, floors, they are my specialty, doors, windows, . . . if I could put myself in a room that would be the end of the wordygurdy" (p. 399). Even his beloved things—the pebbles, boots, and bicycle horns—must go. Beckett has so successfully disavailed himself of imagistic crutches that even the color of the piece, despite the big red eye and the occasional yellows, is grey. And even this is open to question: "perhaps I am the prey, on the subject of grey, in the grey, to delusions" (p. 301).

The attack on space and time is quite a formal achievement. It nonetheless falls short of the speaker's objective: an objective, it would appear, which can be manifested only by silence. The notion of a literature striving for silence has certainly received wide publicity and comment during the last decade, but I know of no one who has explained the necessity of this paradox quite so clearly as the speaker of *The Unnamable*. The paradox arises from two facts. The first is that all words, coming as they do from the world of rational constructs, will quickly lead us back to that world if we employ them. They form little wedges in which everything else is implied—the novels, the newspaper stories, the psychiatrists' reports—in short, the "old irresistible balcony": "But my dear man, come, be reasonable, look, this is you, look at this photograph, and here's your file, no convictions, I assure you, come now, make an effort, at your age, to have no identity, it's a scandal" (p. 377). Names, no matter how humble, represent an insidious threat. Even pronouns cannot be trusted: "it's the fault of the pronouns, there is no name for me, no pronoun for me, all the trouble comes from that" (p. 404). The first person is "really too red a herring" (p. 343). For almost nine pages (355–363) the speaker actually leaps into the third person, hoping that in his absence whatever was represented by the false "I" may flower in silence and be himself. When he returns, impatient, it is to discover nothing new: "But not too fast, it's too soon, to return, to where I am, empty-handed, in triumph, to where I'm waiting, calm, passably calm, knowing, thinking I know, that nothing has befallen me, nothing will befall me, nothing good, nothing bad, nothing to be the death of me, nothing to be the life of me, it would be premature" (p. 363).

The other fact is that there is nothing else but words. Mind, for lack of a better term, is words, words that refuse to stop: "It's entirely a matter of voices, no other image is appropriate." Knowing is verbalizing. The situation, then, once these two facts are acknowledged, is this: that to know himself the speaker must not know it. What he seeks is knowledge of the unnamable, which exists in the absence of words, hence in the absence of knowledge: "To think of me eavesdropping, me, when the silence falls!" (p. 352). This is why even the project of Worm is doomed: "I'm Worm, no, if I were Worm I wouldn't know it, I wouldn't say it, I wouldn't say anything, I'd be Worm" (p. 347). After the Mahood disaster, the speaker is very careful in contriving his new container. Like the circus clown who tries to retrieve his hat, each time kicking it out of reach, he runs through a great battery of approaches: the leap, the softsell, the approach from the rear, the approach in disguise. "Perhaps it's by trying to be Worm that I'll finally succeed in being Mahood, I hadn't thought of that. Then all I'll have to do is be Worm. Which no doubt I shall achieve by trying to be Jones. Then all I'll have to do is be Jones. Stop, perhaps he'll spare me that, have compassion and let me stop. . . . Worm, Worm, it's between the three of us now, and the devil take the hindmost" (p. 339). As Bernal points out, "Le titre de ce roman n'est pas le silence mais l'innommable, c'est-à-dire une région entre les mots et le silence, entre le langage qui ne représente pas et le silence qui est irreprésentable." [5]

Of still greater importance now than ever is that the speaker nurture his incompetence. He must school himself to unlearn all the slick parlance of well-socialized beings, for it is what keeps him from knowledge of himself. He brings to his task the very finest artillery of Beckett's artistry of failure: "My inability to absorb, my genius for forgetting, are more than they reckoned with. Dear incomprehension, it's thanks to you I'll be myself, in the end" (p. 325). Needless to say, his stupidity and the stupidity with which he endows Worm are not sufficient, and he fails once again. This experiment and that of the *Texts* brought Beckett to the famous impasse of the fifties: "At the end of my work there's nothing but dust—the namable. In the last book— 'L'Innommable'—there's complete disintegration. No 'I' no 'have' no 'being.' No nominative, no accusative, no verb. There's no way to go on." [6]

We have discussed the formal attack on time and space and the main facts that are the source of all the speaker's woe. But we have yet to take up the greatest formal achievement of both *The Unnamable* and *Texts for Nothing*—I refer to the text itself. Without story, without people, without things, without space and time, the books become their words and syntax. It is here that we get the direct attempt to imitate in form the experience the speaker is going through. It is through sheer words and syntax, particularly the latter, that each book, as Fletcher says, "imposes its pain on the reader." [7] Therefore, it is in these books that the kind of analysis Cohn performed in her book *Samuel Beckett: The Comic Gamut* is most in order. I shall not duplicate her work here, but I would like to point out what in my opinion are four of the most effective devices Beckett employs at this level.

1. Absurd hypothesis. This is not a method of an-

swering, for the speaker knows in advance that his questions have no answers. Being fully preposterous, his hypotheses do not point toward conclusion or solution but rather reflect back on the situation that gave rise to them, enlarging its incredible nature rather than diminishing it. This is a primary source of the "pain" Mr. Fletcher refers to: given the presence of a continuous stream of questions, we expect prose to try to lead us to or toward answers, whereas in these works the prose simply leads us back to the questions. On the subject of questions itself, for example, the speaker gives us a fine illustration: "But fie these are questions again. That is typical. I know no more questions and they keep on pouring out of my mouth. I think I know what it is, it's to prevent the discourse from coming to an end, this futile discourse which is not credited to me and brings me not a syllable nearer silence" (p. 307). His theological speculations contain perhaps the finest examples of this mode: "To be on the watch and never sight, to listen for the moan that never comes, that's not a life worth living either. And yet it's theirs. He is there, says the master, somewhere, do as I tell you, bring him before me, he's lacking to my glory" (p. 368). Here are two more examples from the *Texts:*

> What's the matter with my head, I must have left it in Ireland, in a saloon, it must be there still, lying on the bar, it's all it deserved.[8]

> it's always evening, why is that, why is it always evening, I'll say why, so as to have said it, have it behind me, an instant.[9]

2. Cancellation. Cancellation follows no simple rule. Often it can be compounded, as in "When now? Unquestioning." Sometimes the statement is perfectly logical, yet the phrasing bestows the unsettling appearance of nonsense upon the statement, as in "off it goes on" in

which the logical sense must do battle with the blatant opposition of "off" and "on." Sometimes it occurs in gentle puns: "He passes, motionless" or "you may even believe yourself dead on condition you make no bones about it." [10] Elsewhere, it often amounts to a simple afterthought that flatly refutes what precedes it: "I seem to speak, it is not I, about me, it is not about me" (p. 291). By combining them in series, Beckett can develop a regular fanfare of negation:

> Suddenly, no, at last, long last, I couldn't any more, I couldn't go on. Someone said, You can't stay here. I couldn't stay there and I couldn't go on. I'll describe the place, that's unimportant. . . . Glorious prospect, but for the mist that blotted out everything, valleys, loughs, plain and sea. . . . I could have stayed in my den, snug and dry, I couldn't. My den, I'll describe it, no, I can't. It's simple, I can do nothing anymore, that's what you think. [11]

3. The analysis of words. The book being of words and about words, the validity of words is constantly open to question. The form in which this technique most commonly occurs is in the sudden discovery that a word in use is not really understood at all: "Keep going, going on, call that going, call that on" (p. 291); "It, say it, not knowing what" (p. 291). The words analyzed are almost always the most common words. They are words the reader takes for granted and the surprise reference is, if not enlightening, at least and as always, unsettling.

4. The incomplete sentence. Toward the end of *The Unnamable*, when the sentences become very long, they change direction many times in a maze of clauses before the period. In other places where the sentence ultimately makes grammatical sense, there still may be the suggestion of a lost subject. The agent here is a

masterly incompetence in the handling of clauses. There is a fine example on the first page of *The Unnamable:* "Can it be that one day, off it goes on, that one day I simply stayed in, in where, instead of going out, in the old way, out to spend day and night as far away as possible, it wasn't far" (p. 291). Because of the cluster of intervening phrases, the bald statement "it wasn't far" appears at war with "as far away as possible," while in fact he is making the logical statement that he stayed "in where . . . it wasn't far." Forgetting to add the question mark helps considerably.[12] "When I think," the narrator of the *Texts* begins, "no, that won't work, when come those who knew me, perhaps even know me still, by sight of course, or by smell, it's as though, it's as if, come on, I don't know, I shouldn't have begun."[13] Usually the agent is a compound of the narrator's inability to control the forward rush of phrases together with his incredibly bad memory: "The fact would seem to be, if in my situation one may speak of facts, not only that I shall have to speak of things of which I cannot speak, but also, which is even more interesting, but also that I, which is if possible even more interesting, that I shall have to, I forget, no matter" (p. 291).

These are disturbing books, both to read and to talk about. One can try to discern patterns or discover some overall shape, but I think the effort is misguided. It is no less misguided than trying to breathe life into the sorry tale of Mahood. Like it or not, they are "solely a matter of voices." Their formal achievements occur at the molecular level of their prose. Yet once we relinquish our expectations of something else and accept these books for what they are, they become an altogether more satisfying experience. It helps, too, to remember that the author is distinct from his creations. However much the speaker may be seeking the unnamable in these works, Beckett the artist is not—just as the artist is not concerned with expressing silence. His task is to present the search, and this he has

er Worlds: The Artist As
netary Engineer

for Nothing was not Beckett's last attempt at a imitation in form of disorder and mystery. The ment *From an Abandoned Work,* published in 1957, vs that he must have intermitted his dramatic work some time afterward with similar fictional experintation. The forward progress of its narrator provides good a model as any for the violent juxtaposition of pposites which characterizes so much of Beckett's ther work. "All was slow," he says, "and then these lashes."[1] No median range is possible: "Now the jog trot on the other hand, I could no more do that than I could fly." To make matters worse, his terrific sprints come at random, like the sudden rages that break his calm. His rages in turn are unrelated to his feelings of violence: "some days I would be feeling violent all day and never have a rage, other days quite quiet for me and have four or five. No, there's no accounting for it, there's no accounting for anything, with a mind like the one I always had, always on the alert against itself."[2]

Nothing could be in greater contrast than the physical and emotional progress of the narrator who followed in 1961. In *How It Is* what extremes there are never conflict; rather, they are contained in a perfect harmony of cause and effect. Crawling and resting, panting and murmuring flash on and off with the regularity of a neon sign. Opposites are perfectly coordinated: "My vertex

done through imitative form: through the destruction of formal implications of time and space and the creation of a prose of cancellation and omission.

It could, however, be argued that by so doing Beckett has at least produced a version of self—not the self the speaker seeks, but perhaps the last expressible. This is the self as process—a constant evolution and devolution of thoughts and questions. As the speaker notes at one point, the mistake he often makes is "to speak of him as if he really existed, in a specific place, whereas the whole thing is no more than a project for the moment" (p. 371). And the self becomes a series of projects for as many moments. The speaker chooses and rejects many hypotheses that come close to leaving it at that. One is particularly appropriate:

> Perhaps that's what I feel, an outside and an inside and me in the middle, perhaps that's what I am, the thing that divides the world in two, on the one side the outside, on the other the inside, that can be as thin as foil, I'm neither one side nor the other, I'm in the middle, I'm the partition, I've two surfaces and no thickness, perhaps that's what I feel, myself vibrating, I'm the tympanum, on the one hand the mind, on the other the world, I don't belong to either. [P. 383]

He rejects it, of course, as he must, but it is essentially what *we* get. We experience the subtle vibrations of the tympanum, the evocation of which is no mean achievement.

There is another reason for accepting these books for what they are: they then become an altogether more pleasant experience. So far we have stressed the "pain" the reader experiences, a pain arising largely from the short-circuiting of expectations. But the same process results in surprise—for which a better term is delight. Even if, in the aforementioned instance, the reader can find no pleasure in the speaker's forgetfulness, he must admit that the phrases that cause the forgetting are delightful: "but also, which is even more interesting, but also that I, which if possible is even more interesting." I mention this partly because it is so easy to forget that these works are highly amusing while one is engaged in the labor of trying to come to terms with them critically.

It is also important to bring this up because Beckett's humor and poise are, after all, rather extraordinary presences in what pretends to be a literary disaster. In an accommodation of the mess, we are getting not only the mess but something quite different—a sense of perfection. The author's control seems absolutely assured in everything from the aside—"it is always well to try and find out what one is talking about" (p. 361)—to the humor of extended imaginings—as, for example, Mahood's in the jar:

> Though not exactly in order I am tolerated by the police. They know I am speechless and consequently incapable of taking unfair advantage of my situation to stir up the population against its governors, by means of burning oratory during the rush hour or subversive slogans whispered, after nightfall, to belated pedestrians the worse for drink. And since I have lost all my members, with the exception of the one time virile, they know also that I shall not be guilty of any gestures liable to be construed as inciting to alms, a prisonable offense. [P. 327]

It is Beckett's classical assurance, the flawlessness of his romanticism, which I find fascinating. If he has failed as no other romantic artist dared fail, it is in more ways than simply the extremity of his failure. For he has also managed his failure far more skillfully.

I speak of a "sense" of perfection. It points up one of the ironies one always comes up against in reading

Beckett: that
failure contin
ett's awareness
symmetry that
ment:

8

> Where now
> Unquestioning.
> Keep
> call that g
> Can it be that one day,
> I simply stayed in, in wher

This is, if you will, a "formal"
set that the speaker's project is
speaker seeks lies outside all not
all knowledge. Form, no matter h
is ordering. Formal disintegratio
fiercely pursued, still eventuates in
acknowledged in 1956, his methods
and formal disintegration only brought
to the "namable."

Oth
Pl

Texts
direc
frag
sho
for
me
as
o

touches my bottom," as the narrator says. Pim and Bom are one, and victim and tormentor endure their interchanging roles in the same way a coin endures its two sides, the one suffering as little as the other enjoys. "Deterioration of the sense of humour fewer tears too" (p. 18).[3]

I have already described *How It Is* as an evacuation from the ruins of Beckett's work in the fifties. Of course, evacuations are not so unusual in his career; indeed, it would be quite possible to describe each of his works as, in its way, an evacuation from its predecessor. Yet the manner of the evacuation in *How It Is* is nonetheless extraordinary, because formally it appears to repudiate the author's entire development. Thus the man who could not "see any trace of any system anywhere" [4] has written a work in which it is hard to see anything else but system. "It's regulated," "it's mathematical," the narrator keeps pointing out as he describes the social interchange of this world: "at the instant I leave Bem another leaves Pim and let us be at that instant one hundred thousand strong then fifty thousand departures fifty thousand abandoned . . . the same instant always everywhere / at the instant I reach Pim another reaches Bem we are regulated thus" (p. 112). Psychology, too, is regulated: Pim operates in perfect accord with a rigid behaviorism in which nothing more is needed than the principles of positive and negative reinforcement. "It's mechanical."

Even language has been restored to order. Only at first, when one comes on it fresh, does it appear chaotic. The departures from ordinary composition—the absence of punctuation and elimination of all but the most necessary words—are to the end of re-creating murmuring, not babbling. Each prose stanza can be broken down into perfectly intelligible units, each in turn containing what the transformational grammarian would call "deep structure." There is no direct attack on grammatical sense as there often is in *The Unnamable*.

In addition, Beckett appears to go out of his way to underscore the repudiation of his earlier work. On the very first page, for example, the narrator hesitates briefly over an old problem: "me if it's me no question impossible too weak no importance." He brings it up only once again a few pages later: "if it's me no question too weak no interest" (pp. 21–22). What he does in these remarks is dispose of the very question that constantly tormented the speaker of *The Unnamable*. The problem of who he really is may be impossible to solve, but it is also irrelevant. In this new fictional world he is a given integer in a perfect mathematical system, or, if you will, part of a machine and easily defined in terms of his relationships to all the other moving parts. Bleak as this world is, the narrator is nonetheless at home in it, among the numbered, and as such is quite different from his predecessors.

You will recall, too, that one of the favorite pastimes of Beckett's earlier creatures—particularly those of the trilogy—was announcing programs. Nothing so distinguished these programs as their lack of fulfillment. Molloy never did get to "draw up the inventory of his goods and possessions," [5] and we hardly need his own admission to know that he "made a balls of" his report. Malone says he is going to tell us four stories: "one about a man, another about a woman, a third about a thing and finally one about an animal, a bird probably." [6] This plan is immediately revised to three stories, to be followed by his inventory, and it is hard to say whether he ends up telling one or two stories. The inventory, inserted before the end, is incomplete. The speaker of *The Unnamable* has his plans too; the audacity of one will stand for many: "Of Worm, at last. Good. We must first, to begin with, go back to his beginnings and then, to go on with, follow him patiently through the various stages, taking care to show their fatal concatenation, which have made him what I am. The whole to be tossed off with bravura. Then notes from day to day, until I collapse. And finally, to wind up with, song and dance of thanksgiving by victim, to celebrate his nativity. Please God nothing goes wrong." [7] Of course, it is the very hopelessness of the programs which provide an index of their importance in these works, for the narrators are obsessed with ordering what will never yield to order. Turning to *How It Is,* we find that its narrator has his program too ("before Pim with Pim after Pim how it is three parts"). The program, however, not only works, but the narrator continually reminds us that it is indeed unfolding according to schedule. He is, in this regard, a very accomplished craftsman. He does what he says he is going to do. In fact, matter and program are so perfectly coordinated that the narrator seems to be contained by a fusion of the two. He is as much crawling toward Part Two as he is toward Pim.

Having described the evacuation, can we account for it? What is Beckett's mimetic intention, if indeed he has one? To begin with it should be noted that there is considerable critical support for the position that *How It Is* is indeed about how it is. As one critic has written: "Man's suffering, cruelty, and loneliness have never found a more desolating metaphor." [8] Others have made similar interpretations:

> Life is the old, traditional, and ruthless voyage; briefly, a couple may be formed, and then the voyage continues in solitude, until there is another brief coupling, with the partners reversing their roles. In spite of that reversal, in spite of a straight-line momentum, and although he may deny it, man keeps going round in circles, repeating a few ridiculous phrases, a few ridiculous gestures.[9]

> The moral judgment . . . behind which the book lines itself up is as clear as it is bleak: Beckett's intention would seem to be to say that, though life

141

in the human city is comprised of manifold relations, they all move within the single polarity involving torturer and victim, both roles being enacted in turn by all men in the various relations with one another into which they are brought by the adventures of life.[10]

What these critics agree upon is that the book bears direct witness to the true plight of man: if we peel away all that is "above in the light" (which seems in this interpretation to include those outer layers of our personality which make us complex and unique), we shall discover "how it is," that our needs are "sustenance and murmuring," that we alternately move and rest, that we are alternately victims and tormentors, that we wish (perhaps) to love and to be loved, that our progress is slow and our activities inevitable.

Yet if we take the title of this work at face value, we must in turn postulate a radical change in the Beckett world view. We must have him admit as reality what he had argued so strenuously in his essay on Proust was only the fabrication of Memory and Habit. Mystery is thus drained from the universe as is, so the narrator points out, its comedy and tears. I think it more likely then, particularly in light of the way Beckett labors to underscore the differences between *How It Is* and its forebears, that the title is in fact a monumental joke.

Not that we should read the book with hilarity, but something that at times approaches it: "victim of number 4 at A enroute along AB tormentor of number 2 at B abandoned again but this time at B victim again of number 4 but this time at B enroute again but this time along BA tormentor of number 2 again but this time at A and finally abandoned again at A and all set to begin again" (p. 118). It is all quite absurd, but absurd now in the sense that it has nothing to do with how it is. "If there were only darkness, all would be clear. It is because there is not only darkness but also light that our situation becomes inexplicable." [11] In *How It Is*, Beckett has reduced it all to darkness—to clarity.

"Life above in the light" is our world or, in other words, how it is. Its intrusions in the form of "rags" or images are, therefore, the chaotic, unrelated elements in the novel. It is the place of disorder and emotion, and also of injustice, as the narrator points out in a parody of the parable of the sheep: "to his eyes the spectacle on the one hand of a single one among us towards whom no one ever goes and on the other of a single other who never goes towards anyone it would be an injustice and that is above in the light" (p. 124). Down here, naturally, justice is perfect. The victims "triumph if only narrowly" in being allowed motion. The tormentors must lie still: "penalty perhaps of their recent exertions but effect also of our justice" (p. 143).

In 1959 Beckett published a short piece entitled "L'Image," [12] in which the narrator, face down in the mud with his sack, constructs a touching image of himself as a youth in the country with his sweetheart and dog—"pâles cheveux en brosse grosse face rouge avec boutons ventre débordant braguette béante jambes cagneuses en fuseau écartées pour plus d'assise fléchissant aux genoux pieds ouverts cent trente-cinq degrés." The passage is actually a series of images in which impressions come in confusing, disconnected flashes. In its essentials (though with extensive stylistic revisions) the piece was incorporated in *Comment c'est* where it appears as one of the rags of life above in the light. Following, as it did, *From an Abandoned Work* [13] and containing no hint of the fabulous system of *Comment c'est*, "L'Image," I would suspect, represents a last effort in the mimesis of disorder Beckett had been struggling with in his prose for most of his artistic career.

The solution to his problem, then, lay in rejecting both incompetence and imitative form as artistic methods and adopting what is in part, at least, a satire of competence cast in the guise of otherworldly exploration.

143

Instead of taking the direct route to how it is, he went in the other direction and defined it by how it is not. Thus what Beckett composed in *How It Is* was a *reductio ad absurdum* of the human demand for order set in a Newtonian afterlife. "I always loved arithmetic," the narrator says, "it has paid me back in full" (p. 37). His crime is his rage for order, and his rage for order is reflected in the thought patterns of the race: "it's not said where on earth I can have received my education acquired my notions of mathematics astronomy and even physics they have marked me that's the main thing" (p. 41). These notions, to which the earth never yielded, are now the pattern for creation; having a perfect omniscience and omnipotence, the narrator is the supremely successful classical artist. He fabricates a clockwork afterlife in the image of his own mind, old and vast enough to contain both expiation and reward.

The sin for which the narrator suffers—that of yielding to the rage for order—is to be found in everyone. But the narrator must suffer for us all and, hence, must have a superhuman competence—one capable of sustaining the entire verbal fabric of *How It Is*. He is also its creator, taking for his pattern the ideal form of what is latent in everyman, and hence creating and existing in that for which everyman is responsible. It only remains for him to die for the world, and in dying to harrow this unearthly paradise. He does so, needless to say, with his arms spread "like a cross." The act of sacrifice is the act of denial. His heroism lies in the terrific effort of will required, after the final calculations have been made and all parts accounted for, to say that it is "all balls."

It should be mentioned at this point that there are other critics who by different routes have arrived at conclusions as extreme as this. Fletcher, for example, has written that in reading *How It Is* "we are spectators at a ballet, formal and untroubled by any reality but its own, by any principle but that, inevitable and

144

serene, of its own growth and rapid decline." [14] Federman has argued that "this novel is not a projection of reality, but an experiment in willful artistic failure: the rejection of reality. . . . *Comment c'est* is a world of abstractions and illusions which poses as fiction, just as conventional fiction pretends to pass for reality." [15]

Can we, however, depart so radically from the critical opinion we quoted previously? After all, Beckett did call his novel *How It Is*. And if one takes it as a joke, one must remember that almost all Beckett's jokes can be taken in more than one way. Indeed, though the book represents a radical *formal* departure, the materials it employs are still highly familiar. As one critic has noted: "This world contains no ingredient (unless perhaps mud) which we have not encountered before." [16] The need for sustenance and the need to "commit words," motion and rest, torment and tormenting, and "good moments somehow or other": these are basic ingredients—basic to how it is—and Beckett has never avoided them. They are as fundamental to the works charting the possible disorder as they are to the work charting the impossible order. In this work, as in the others, the basic ingredients seem especially true in the way in which they have been reduced. Pim and Bom are in the great tradition of Hairy Mac and Sucky Moll. What is compelling is Beckett's ability to deromanticize. [17]

In addition to these "basic ingredients," it can also be granted that Beckett is showing us how it is with our imagination. Beckett may be in the dark as to where mind and body meet, but there seems little doubt that he includes both mind and matter in whatever reality is. Here we not only have an imagination but we have one working on principles of order that, though they may plague us, are in a real sense very much *with* us. If the portrait of mind is fictional, it is so in the best sense of the word; for it makes brilliantly clear the condition of mind that is common to man. What Beckett may well have concluded when he abandoned his experiments in disintegration is that there is absolutely no dissociating either form or mind from order. Thus although the method Beckett employed in the trilogy was disintegration, every step in the process of disintegration depended on some idea of order for its effect. The finer the separation of part from part, the more exquisite the sense of order assumed. The problem, in short, was the reverse of what it appeared—not form disintegrating, but the impossibility of disintegrating form.

What we have, then, in *How It Is* are the parts of how it is—matter and mind. In their purest forms—the mud and the voice—their reality is acknowledged even at the end when the narrator annihilates all the rest.

What we do *not* have is how it is: how the parts combine without relation and cohere without order.

Very near the end of *How It Is*, the narrator entertains the possibility of another creation:

> and if it is still possible at this late hour to conceive of other worlds

> as just as ours but less exquisitely organized

> one perhaps there is one perhaps somewhere merciful enough to shelter such frolics where no one ever abandons anyone and no one ever waits for anyone and never two bodies touch [P. 143]

This possibility is realized in almost every detail in the seven-page work *Imagination Dead Imagine*, though this planet is abandoned, too: "Leave them there, sweating and icy, there is better elsewhere." [18] *Imagination Dead Imagine* appears at once more ambitious and more modest than *How It Is*. It Pretends, as it were, to understand the disaster that preceded it, to be more scrupulous, more limited, more scientific. This is its guise: a rigidly controlled search for that arrangement of matter which is both ordered *and* representative of how it is. The implied hope is that, once the list of basic ingredients has been sufficiently reduced, the common denominator of matter and mind will prove to be order. The narrator follows a process of elimination "to find a form that accommodates the mess," [19] to determine, in other words, how much of the mess can be accommodated by form.

The work opens before imagination has exerted control, the counters of fancy welling up out of the whiteness of the page: "Islands, waters, azure, verdure." Then, as if in dictation, we are told to "omit," for these have no hope of being accommodated. The inventory that required so elaborate, and hence preposterous, a form in *How It Is* is then drastically reduced so that it might be accommodated by a simpler form that will not falsify how it is. The form that is allowed to take shape is of the most elementary symmetry. It contains man and woman (back to back like a reversed Yin and Yang) breathing, perspiring, and murmuring "ah"; they are in a rotunda that can be womb and tomb as well as the mind that imagines them ("a ring as in the imagination the ring of bone"); and they suffer the same ebb and flow of light and heat that man suffers in his days and seasons.

As the narrator of *How It Is* predicted, though, this world is "less exquisitely organized" than his. Between the calms of extreme white and heat and extreme black and cold are pauses of varying length with attendant vibrations and occasional reversals of direction—all variations "combining in countless rhythms." Part of the flux, then, has been included; but only so much as can be contained in the symmetry of form: "whatever its uncertainties the return sooner or later to a temporary calm seems assured, for the moment, in the black dark or the great whiteness, with attendant temperature, world still proof against enduring tumult."

Order is even more seriously threatened by changes of time outside the cycles of seasons and days. For this reason the book, like many of Beckett's works, has a shorter second act. It begins without warning in the solid block of words ("Rediscovered miraculously after what absence in perfect voids . . ."). In this second half, though the perfectly symmetrical image of the womb-tomb remains, we discover that the rest "is no longer the same." The bodies have become distinguishable, the hair has grown white, the eyes open, the lips murmur "ah," and the sense of tumult has increased: "briefer lulls and never twice the same storm."

Finally, the form, it is confessed, is valid only "for the moment." There is no telling whether in the future they will "lie still in the stress of that storm, or of a worse storm, or in the black dark for good, or the great whiteness unchanging," for the validity of the form depends on the source of light and heat, "of which still no trace." We have no way of knowing when He "in charge of the sacks," as the narrator of *How It Is* called Him, will choose not to yield to the humblest of forms. "Leave them there," the narrator says, "sweating and icy, there is better elsewhere." And, though he immediately follows this statement with "no, there is nothing elsewhere," his desire to find "better elsewhere" is understandable, since what is pitiable about *Imagination Dead Imagine* is the meagerness of the prey. Beckett ironically underlines this meagerness by his continual measurement and testing:

> Diameter three feet, three feet from ground to summit of the vault. Two diameters at right angles AB CD divide the white ground into two semicircles ACB BDA.

> Go back out, a plain rotunda, all white in the whiteness, go back in, rap, solid throughout.

Hold a mirror to their lips, it mists.

It is as if to say, "This order is no spurious one, for it contains these realities."

Beckett has not yet abandoned his work in planetary engineering. Very recently he published approximately fifty pages entitled *Le Dépeupleur*.[20] Like *How It Is* and *Imagination Dead Imagine* it is a Dantean epic in miniature, ringed and self-contained. Its design is of consummate mathematical exactitude: a cylinder, fifty meters in circumference by sixteen in height, resting on the earth, capped at the top. Within, the cylinder is lit throughout by vibrating yellow light. The temperature ranges from five to twenty-five degrees, oscillating from high to low to high again over eight-second intervals. All variations of light and temperature cease at rare intervals for about ten seconds. The cylinder is populated by one body per square meter or in round figures two hundred bodies. The bodies are divided into four categories, of which three are seekers ("cherchant chacun son dépeupleur") and the fourth are "non-chercheurs" or better "ex-chercheurs" who sit for the most part against the wall (in the attitude, the author notes, which evoked from Dante one of his rare smiles). There are also ladders, about fifteen, resting at various points against the wall of the cylinder, used for two purposes: simply to get off the ground or to climb up into caves that riddle the upper part of the wall. Some of these caves are connected by tunnels. The behavior of the seekers is governed by certain laws pertaining to time allowed in the caves, access to the ladders, investigation of bodies, and other matters. These and numerous other details and refinements are carefully blueprinted in fifteen paragraphs, each paragraph devoted to an aspect of the world, the last dealing with the time just preceding "l'impensable fin si cette notion est maintenue."

It would appear that Beckett has pushed his indulgence in planetary design to an extreme. There are no memories to haunt this creator. Like the creator of *Imagination Dead Imagine,* he stands outside his creation. There is no need to destroy it, to say that it is "all balls." No need even to leave it in search of better worlds. It is a kind of game now. Yet, as in the games of Malone, ages ago, the escape to another planet is a return to our own.

When Dante the poet constructed a universe of radiant symmetry, he sent Dante the fictive agent to explore it. This was because the formal brilliance of his creation was in the service of mysteries beyond man's intelligence. The omniscient genius had to humble himself and follow guides through his handiwork. Beckett's omniscient construction is also cast as a "séjour." This world of universally classifiable parts and movements operates for the keener perception of mysteries of our world. In the cylinder, for example, there are two beliefs concerning the possibility of an "issue": one, that it lies in a yet to be discovered passage leading off from one of the tunnels; the other, that it lies in a trapdoor hidden in the ceiling. The first naturally becomes less tenable as time goes on, while the second, unfortunately, cannot be tested because of rules governing the emplacement of ladders. All that is new here and on the surface curious, augments the strangeness of all that is old—as in this instance, the familiar mystery of "issue." Conversely, all that is invented and extraordinary is clear, knowable, even tedious. Yes, a cylinder, full of people, with ladders and caves, the walls like India rubber. Yet this precise but alien detail allows us to discover again the difficulty of accounting for our own world. The cylinder *appears* to exist for the conversion of bodies from seekers to nonseekers, perhaps finally to dust. One calls it a "Dépeupleur."

In *Watt,* Beckett employs the phrase, "great formal brilliance and indeterminable import." It would be possible to argue that these two qualities have, in one way or another, always coexisted in Beckett's work, but that in *Watt* and the trilogy, Beckett most assiduously cultivated the "indeterminable import" while in the drama and recent fiction he cultivated the "great formal brilliance." Thus, descriptions of great formal brilliance in the earlier work were agents of depthless confusion:

> Mr. Fitzwein looked at Mr. Magershon, on his right. But Mr Magershon is not looking at Mr Fitzwein, on his left, but at Mr O'Meldon, on his right. But Mr O'Meldon is not looking at Mr. Magershon, on his left, but, craning forward, at Mr MacStern, on his left but three at the far end of the table. But Mr MacStern . . .[21]

How often does this formula recur in Beckett's stage directions! Yet on stage it releases performances of stark symmetry:

> After a moment they join hands as follows: Vi's right hand with Ru's right hand, Vi's left hand with Flo's left hand, Flo's right hand with Ru's left hand, Vi's arms being above Ru's left arm and Flo's right arm. The three pairs of clasped hands rest on the three laps.
>
> Silence [22]

It is quite likely that the new directions I have been discussing arose in one way or another as a consequence of Beckett's work in drama. Alec Reid's comments on the comparative virtues of drama and fiction are very suggestive in this regard:

> Beckett finds that writing a play is quite different from writing a novel. It is easier, more relaxed. This may seem surprising, but the reason is simple

enough. When a man writes a piece for performance in a theatre, he at once subjects himself to certain external requirements. He must so construct his play that the actors can be seen and heard, and he must mould it into some framework of acts and scenes. Such limitations are the basic rules of the game, and if they are not observed the piece cannot be performed. With the novel, however, it is quite different; the author has complete liberty. He can abandon a character whenever he likes, he need not even finish a sentence or ever trouble himself about a paragraph. The only limitations are those which he imposes upon himself. Beckett says that when he sets out to write a novel, he is entering a jungle, an area of utter lawlessness where no rules of any sort apply, and that he finds the change to working on a play like coming out of night into light.[23]

Designing other planets was obviously another way of getting out of the jungle, a way of going beyond imitative form, of reasserting law and order, without sacrificing mimetic integrity. Its obsessively systematic character does not validate the Newtonian universe. It is controlled from afar, by what it is not—the life it fails to imitate, which in its turn receives some validation from what it is not. It is one example of the "new form" Beckett spoke of in his interview with Driver: "form . . . of such a type that it admits the chaos and does not say that the chaos is really something else. The form and the chaos remain separate. The latter is not reduced to the former." [24]

It is hard to write a book with a beginning, middle, and end on Beckett. I have tried, delineating three major stages—early, middle, and late—in Beckett's approach to form in fiction. Having traced his development and rejection of imitative form, my study comes to its proper end. But Beckett is still writing. What is now "late" promises to become "middle late," perhaps in time "late middle." In other work published in the sixties, what still impresses is the variety of formal experiment and the autonomy of each endeavor. *Enough,* which was published in French the year after *Imagination Dead Imagine,* appears to be primarily lyrical in intention: a haunting evocation of loss, strangely made more poignant by its utterly bizarre fictional detail. *Ping* (*Bing,* 1966) and *Lessness* (*Sans,* 1967) are even more radically different. In these Beckett may well have gone beyond the province of fiction altogether, perhaps to a species of poetry in which form imitates neither this world nor another, but functions affectively as rhythm and genetically as discipline. They lie beyond the scope of this study, but they show that Beckett, in his sixties, is still vigorous and inventive.

Notes

INTRODUCTION

[1] Samuel Beckett, "La Peinture des Van Velde," *Les Cahiers d'art,* 21 (1945–1946), 349.

[2] Beckett, *Happy Days* (New York: Grove Press, 1961), pp. 42–43.

[3] Alec Reid, *All I Can Manage, More than I Could: An Approach to the Plays of Samuel Beckett* (Dublin: Dolmen Press, 1968), p. 48.

[4] Susan Sontag, *Against Interpretation and Other Essays* (New York: Farrar, Straus and Giroux, 1966), p. 14.

[5] John Fletcher, *Samuel Beckett's Art* (New York: Barnes and Noble, 1967), p. 12.

[6] Beckett *Proust* (New York: Grove Press, 1957), pp. 53–54.

[7] "Beckett's Letters on 'Endgame': Extracts from his Correspondence with Alan Schneider," *The Village Voice,* 19 March 1958, p. 15.

[8] Beckett, *Proust,* p. 62.

[9] *Ibid.,* p. 61.

[10] Olga Bernal, *Langage et fiction dans le roman de Beckett* (Paris: Gallimard, 1969), pp. 131–132.

[11] Samuel Beckett and Georges Duthuit, "Three Dialogues," *in* Martin Esslin ed. *Samuel Beckett: A Collection of Critical Essays* (Englewood Cliffs, N.J.: Prentice-Hall, 1965), p. 21.

[12] Reid, *All I Can Manage,* p. 53.

[13] Yvor Winters, *In Defense of Reason* (Denver: Alan Swallow, 1947), p. 64n.

[14] R. P. Blackmur, *Form and Value in Modern Poetry* (Garden City: Doubleday, 1957), p. 256.

[15] This does not mean, of course, that the two concepts are mutually exclusive. For example, "the Whitmanian notion that one must write loose and sprawling poetry to 'express' the loose and sprawling American continent" [Winters, *In Defense of Reason,* p. 144], when put into practice by Whitman is an example at once of both concepts for the simple reason that Whitman identified himself with his country. One may, however, hold the same "Whitmanian notion" and not compose in the more or less unconscious manner of the "expressive" artist. I can imagine, for example, an artist casting about deliberately for formal devices that he feels are most imitative of his country.

155

[16] Lawrence Harvey, "Art and the Existential in *Waiting for Godot*," *PMLA*, 75 (March 1960), 137–146.

[17] "Beckett's Letters on 'Endgame,'" p. 15.

[18] Stanley Cavell, *Must We Mean What We Say? A Book of Essays* (New York: Scribner, 1969), p. 152.

[19] Alan Schneider, "Waiting for Beckett: a personal chronicle," *Chelsea Review*, no. 2 (September 1958), p. 7.

[20] Martin Esslin, *The Theatre of the Absurd* (Garden City: Doubleday, 1961), p. xx. Sartre himself called for a revolution in literary form in *What is Literature?* (New York: Harper and Row, 1965), p. 223, making an implicit deduction from what is essentially a version of imitative form: "We hope that our books remain in the air all by themselves and that their words, instead of pointing backwards toward the one who has designed them, will be toboggans, forgotten, unnoticed, and solitary, which will hurl the reader into the midst of a universe where there are no witnesses; in short, that our books may exist in the manner of things, of plants, of events, and not at first like the products of man. We want to drive providence from our works as we have driven it from our world."

[21] Tom F. Driver, "Beckett by the Madeleine," *Columbia University Forum*, 4 (Summer 1961), 23.

[22] Burt Prelusky, "Ultra Violet Ways," *West*, 29 June 1969, p. 4.

[23] Beckett, *Three Novels* (New York: Grove Press, 1965), p. 13.

[24] Driver, "Beckett by the Madeleine," p. 23.

CHAPTER 1: EARLY FICTION

[1] Samuel Beckett, "A Case in a Thousand," *The Bookman*, 86 (August 1934), 241–242.

[2] All numbers in parenthesis in this chapter refer to pages in Beckett, *More Pricks Than Kicks* (London: Chatto and Windus, 1934).

[3] This particular device may be a first inkling of a device Beckett was later to apply to his entire canon. I refer to his disturbing practice of lodging here and there references to figures from his other books. As here he mocks the idea of a coherent novel, so later he mocks the idea of a coherent literary canon.

[4] Dante meets his friend Belacqua in the fourth canto of "Purgatory" (sitting in much the same posture his namesake takes on the curb in "A Wet Night"). Because he delayed repentance so long, he must wait in Purgatory for a time equivalent to his life on earth.

[5] Ruby Cohn, *Samuel Beckett: The Comic Gamut* (New Brunswick, N.J.: Rutgers University Press, 1962), pp. 33–34.

[6] Raymond Federman, "Belacqua and the Inferno of Society," *Journey to Chaos: Samuel Beckett's Early Fiction* (Berkeley and Los Angeles: University of California Press, 1965), pp. 31–55.

[7] Hugh Kenner, *Samuel Beckett: A Critical Study* (New York: Grove Press, 1961), p. 35.

[8] Frederick Hoffman, *Samuel Beckett: The Language of Self* (New York: E. P. Dutton, 1964), p. 101.

CHAPTER 2: BECKETT'S NOVEL

1 All numbers in parenthesis in this chapter refer to pages in Samuel Beckett, *Murphy* (New York: Grove Press [1957]).

2 Hugh Kenner, *Samuel Beckett: A Critical Study* (New York: Grove Press, 1961), p. 75.

3 Raymond Federman, *Journey to Chaos* (Berkeley and Los Angeles: University of California Press, 1965), p. 67.

4 Ludovic Janvier, *Pour Samuel Beckett* (Paris: Éditions de Minuit, 1966), p. 27.

5 The intrusion is handled in even more cavalier fashion in the French translation: "Les termes du passage ci-dessus furent choisis avec soin, lors de la rédaction en anglo-irlandais, afin de corrompre le lecteur cultivé" (Paris: Bordas, 1947), p. 89. This is not the only reference in the French to the book's previous existence in another language.

6 For a much more thorough inventory of misplaced literalisms and variants of clichés, proverbs, and quotations see Ruby Cohn's chapter on *Murphy* in *Samuel Beckett: The Comic Gamut* (New Brunswick, N.J.: Rutgers University Press, 1962).

7 The old boy makes a brief return in *Malone Dies* when Malone calls the roll of his past incarnations: "There was the old butler too, in London I think, there's London again, I cut his throat with his razor" (Beckett, *Three Novels* [New York: Grove Press, 1965], p. 236).

8 Willam York Tindall, *Samuel Beckett* (New York and London: Columbia University Press, 1964), p. 17.

9 *Ibid.*

10 See particularly Maurice Nadeau, "Samuel Beckett: Humor and the Void," *in* Martin Esslin, ed., *Samuel Beckett: A Collection of Critical Essays* (Englewood Cliffs, N.J.: Prentice-Hall, 1965), pp. 33–36; also Federman, *Journey to Chaos*, pp. 83–84.

11 There have been several discussions about the influence of Descartes and the Occasionalists Geulincx and Malebranche on *Murphy*. See particularly Samuel Mintz, "Beckett's *Murphy*: A 'Cartesian' Novel," *Perspective* (Autumn 1959), pp. 156–165; Kenner, "The Rational Domain," *Samuel Beckett*, pp. 79–115; Robert Harrison, *Samuel Beckett's Murphy: A Critical Excursion* (Athens: University of Georgia Press, 1968), pp. 66–68; chapters on *Murphy* in Richard N. Coe, *Samuel Beckett* (New York: Grove Press, 1964) and Federman, *Journey to Chaos*.

12 For the most clearly opposing view to this argument, the reader is referred to Coe's chapter on *Murphy* (*Samuel Beckett*, p. 20). Coe argues: "What am I? What are time and space? What are mind and matter, what is reality? These are the questions which form the substance of Beckett's first novel, *Murphy*."

13 Note that Murphy leaves Ticklepenny "to face the music, MUSIC, MUSIC" after he dies (*ibid.*, p. 252).

14 For more paradigms see Harrison, *Samuel Beckett's Murphy*.

CHAPTER 3: IMITATIVE FORM

¹ All numbers in parentheses in this chapter refer to pages in Samuel Beckett, *Watt* (New York: Grove Press, 1959).

² David H. Hesla, "The Shape of Chaos: A Reading of Beckett's *Watt*," *Critique: Studies in Modern Fiction*, 6 (Spring 1963), 92–93.

³ Ludovic Janvier, *Pour Samuel Beckett* (Paris: Éditions de Minuit, 1966), p. 33.

⁴ Jacqueline Hoefer, *"Watt,"* in Martin Esslin, ed., *Samuel Beckett: A Collection of Critical Essays* (Englewood Cliffs, N.J.: Prentice-Hall, 1965), p. 64.

⁵ For an interesting and thorough analysis of the role of "music" in *Watt*, see Susan Field Senneff, "Song and Music in Samuel Beckett's *Watt*," *Modern Fiction Studies*, 10 (Summer 1964), 137–149.

⁶ Hesla, "Shape of Chaos," p. 103.

⁷ For a fascinating exposition of this subject in terms of the disintegrating relationship between the author and his work, see Olga Bernal's account in *Langage et fiction dans le roman de Beckett* (Paris: Gallimard, 1969), pp. 94–113.

⁸ Hugh Kenner, *Samuel Beckett: A Critical Study* (New York: Grove Press, 1961), p. 23.

⁹ Tom F. Driver, "Beckett by the Madeleine," *Columbia University Forum*, 4 (Summer 1961), 23.

¹⁰ Hesla, "Shape of Chaos," p. 90.

¹¹ *Ibid.*, p. 89.

¹² *Ibid.*, pp. 101–102.

¹³ Ruby Cohn, *Samuel Beckett: The Comic Gamut* (New Brunswick, N.J.: Rutgers University Press, 1962), p. 94.

¹⁴ A more extended application of Arsene's theory to Beckett's humor can be found in Josephine Jacobsen and William R. Mueller, *The Testament of Samuel Beckett* (New York: Hill and Wang, 1964), pp. 87–99.

¹⁵ *Ibid.*, pp. 92–93.

¹⁶ Beckett, *Murphy*, p. 65.

CHAPTER 4: REACTION

¹ See particularly Ruby Cohn, *Samuel Beckett: The Comic Gamut* (New Brunswick, N.J.: Rutgers University Press, 1962), pp. 95–102; John Fletcher, *The Novels of Samuel Beckett* (London: Chatto and Windus, 1964), p. 113; Raymond Federman, *Journey to Chaos* (Berkeley and Los Angeles: University of California Press, 1965), pp. 138–139.

² All numbers in parentheses in this chapter refer to pages in Samuel Beckett, *Mercier et Camier* (Paris: Éditions de Minuit, 1970).

³ See Colin Duckworth's chapter "Godot: Genesis and Composition" in Beckett, *En attendant Godot*, ed. Colin Duckworth (London: George G. Harrap, 1966), pp. xlv–lxxv.

⁴ There is also the possibility that at this time Beckett may have been dissatisfied with *Watt*. I understand from Mr. Kenner, who in turn has it from Beckett, that *Watt* is by no means the author's favorite book.

[5] I infer this from a passage in which Watt strives to convince a policeman that it would be better if Mercier and Camier were allowed to remain in the city: "les néons, les pickpockets, les agents, les bordels, toute l'agitation du Bondy métropolitain, cela les calme et les prédispose à une nuit réparatrice" (p. 197). If this is the actual Bondy then I presume the canal is the Canal de l'Ourcq. It is interesting to note in regard to this that there is a Beckett manuscript in the University of Texas Library entitled *Les Bosquets de Bondy*. It dates from about 1945 and contains some of Beckett's first writing in French.

[6] See also Hugh Kenner, *Samuel Beckett: A Critical Study* (New York: Grove Press, 1961), pp. 70–71, 126–128, 146–149.

[7] I have taken the liberty of providing translations for the longer passages. The translations are my own.

[8] Kenner, *Samuel Beckett*, p. 76.

[9] There has been some temptation among critics to see in the pseudocouple a symbolic figuring of mind and body: Mercier (mind) and Camier (body). Fletcher, on the other hand, finds it "difficult to establish any such neat identification" (*The Novels*, p. 116). I find myself in agreement with Fletcher. Not only is it difficult to make this equation, it is fraught with peril for it makes an allegorical reading almost inevitable.

[10] Kenner, *Samuel Beckett*, p. 76.

[11] Quoted by Duckworth in his Introduction to *En attendant Godot*, p. xlvii.

[12] Fletcher, *The Novels*, p. 118.

Chapter 5: Two Reports

[1] The pseudocouple's exchange brought to my mind the account of a project quoted by Marshall McLuhan in *The Gutenberg Galaxy* (Toronto: University of Toronto Press, 1962), p. 36: "The next bit of evidence was very, very interesting. This man—the sanitary inspector—made a moving picture, in very slow time, very slow technique, of what would be required of the ordinary household in a primitive African village in getting rid of standing water—draining pools, picking up all empty tins and putting them away, and so forth. We showed this film to an audience and asked them what they had seen, and they said they had seen a chicken, a fowl, and we didn't know there was a fowl in it! So we very carefully scanned the frames one by one for this fowl, and, sure enough, for about a second, a fowl went over the corner of the frame. Someone had frightened the fowl and it had taken flight, through the righthand, bottom segment of the frame. This was all that had been seen. The other things he had hoped they would pick up from the film they had not picked up at all, and they had picked up something which we didn't know was in the film until we inspected it minutely."

[2] Maurice Nadeau, "Samuel Beckett: Humor and the Void," in Martin Esslin, ed., *Samuel Beckett: A Collection of Critical Essays* (Englewood Cliffs, N.J.: Prentice-Hall, 1965), p. 33.

3 All numbers in parentheses in this and the next two chapters refer to pages in Samuel Beckett, *Three Novels* (New York: Grove Press, 1965).

4 For a fine exploration of these and other correspondences in *Molloy*, see Ludovic Janvier, *Pour Samuel Beckett* (Paris: Éditions de Minuit, 1966), pp. 48–61.

5 John Fletcher, *The Novels of Samuel Beckett* (London: Chatto and Windus, 1964), p. 132.

6 Going a bit further still, David Hayman argues that "Molloy's mother, Molloy, Moran and Moran's son all inhabit the same body; further, the events described in the two narratives are simultaneous and identical though viewed from different angles and differently ordered. Since the narrators are by their own admission untrustworthy to the point of absurdity, it seems probable that they are actually rationalizing the behavior of a posited third force (Youdi or Jacques Junior?) over whom they have progressively lost their power" (*"Molloy* or The Quest for Meaninglessness: A Global Interpretation," *in* Melvin J. Friedman, ed., *Samuel Beckett Now: Critical Approaches to His Novels, Poetry and Plays* [Chicago: University of Chicago Press, 1970], pp. 135–136).

7 Beckett, *Stories and Texts for Nothing* (New York: Grove Press, 1967), p. 25.

8 *Ibid.,* p. 72.

9 *Ibid.,* p. 27.

10 Quoted by Israel Shenker, "Moody Man of Letters," *New York Times,* 6 May 1956, sec. 2, p. 1.

11 Samuel Beckett and Georges Duthuit, "Three Dialogues," *in* Esslin, ed., *Samuel Beckett*, p. 17.

12 Ruby Cohn, *Samuel Beckett: The Comic Gamut* (New Brunswick, N.J.: Rutgers University Press, 1962), p. 138.

CHAPTER 6: AN EXERCISE-BOOK

1 Samuel Beckett, *Molloy* (Paris: Éditions de Minuit, 1951), p. 9. Later Molloy says, "Yes, let me cry out, this time, then another time perhaps, then perhaps a last time" (25). The French version again predicts only one more utterance: "Oui, crions, cette fois-ci, puis encore une peut-être" (36).

2 John Fletcher, *The Novels of Samuel Beckett* (London: Chatto and Windus, 1964), p. 129.

CHAPTER 7: TEXT

1 Ruby Cohn, *Samuel Beckett: The Comic Gamut* (New Brunswick, N.J.: Rutgers University Press, 1962), p. 175.

2 Frederick Hoffman, *Samuel Beckett: The Language of Self* (New York: E. P. Dutton, 1964), p. 93.

3 John Fletcher, *The Novels of Samuel Beckett* (London: Chatto and Windus, 1964), p. 196.

4 The English text represents a change in the arrangement of these

opening words. The French reads: "Où maintenant? Quand maintenant? Qui maintenant?" Samuel Beckett, *L'Innommable* (Paris: Éditions de Minuit, 1953).

5 Olga Bernal, *Langage et fiction dans le roman de Beckett* (Paris: Gallimard, 1969), pp. 190–191.

6 Israel Shenker, "Moody Man of Letters," *New York Times*, 6 May, 1956, sec. 2, pp. 1, 3.

7 Fletcher, *The Novels of Samuel Beckett*, p. 179.

8 Samuel Beckett, *Stories and Texts for Nothing* (New York: Grove Press, 1967), p. 113. The logic is slightly different in the French where it begins: "il n'y a personne, où ai-je donc la tête. . . ." *Nouvelles et textes pour rien* (Paris: Éditions de Minuit, 1958), p. 185.

9 *Ibid.*, p. 127.

10 *Ibid.*, p. 93.

11 *Ibid.*, p. 75.

12 A calculated omission, not a typographer's error. It is missing in the French as well.

13 Beckett, *Stories and Texts for Nothing*, p. 127.

CHAPTER 8: OTHER WORLDS

1 Samuel Beckett *From an Abandoned Work* (London: Faber and Faber, 1958), p. 13.

2 *Ibid.*, p. 12.

3 Numbers in parentheses refer to pages in Beckett, *How It Is* (New York: Grove Press, 1964).

4 Israel Shenker, "Moody Man of Letters," *New York Times*, 6 May, 1956, sec. 2, p. 3.

5 Beckett, *Three Novels* (New York: Grove Press, 1965), p. 47.

6 *Ibid.*, p. 181.

7 *Ibid.*, p. 352.

8 William York Tindall, *Samuel Beckett* (New York and London: Columbia University Press, 1964), p. 38.

9 Ruby Cohn, *Samuel Beckett: The Comic Gamut* (New Brunswick, N.J.: Rutgers University Press, 1962), pp. 206–207.

10 Nathan A. Scott, *Samuel Beckett* (London: Bowes and Bowes, 1965), p. 78.

11 Tom F. Driver, "Beckett by the Madeleine," *Columbia University Forum*, 4 (Summer 1961), 23.

12 Beckett, "L'Image," *X, A Quarterly Review*, I (November 1959), 35–37.

13 Final version first published in *Evergreen Review*, I, 3 (1957), 83–91. The chronology of publication for these late pieces is as follows: *From an Abandoned Work*, 1957; "L'Image," 1959; *Comment c'est*, 1961 (Paris: Éditions de Minuit). As if to clarify the progression, Beckett published the first translated fragment of *Comment c'est* under the title "From an Unabandoned Work" (*Evergreen Review*, IV [September–October 1961], 58–65).

14 John Fletcher, *The Novels of Samuel Beckett* (London: Chatto and Windus, 1964), pp. 215–216. The phrasings have even more

extreme implications, and Fletcher is carefully tentative in developing them: "Is it too wild a deduction to suppose that this author, despairing completely of saying anything new, feels driven to making things of beauty instead? When 'literature' seems to him sham and farce, a well-produced book perhaps appears a more honourable achievement. The logical consequence of such an attitude would be to esteem the printer and binder above the writer, and this is, in fact, the sort of conclusion before which some artists of our time have shown they do not recoil" (p. 220).

15 Raymond Federman, "How It Is with Beckett's Fiction," *French Review*, 38 (February 1965), 461.

16 Hugh Kenner, *Samuel Beckett: A Critical Study* (New York: Grove Press, 1961), p. 199. The tension in *How It Is* which I am articulating here was, I believe, first observed by Kenner: "In our fascinated affinity with these twilight men, none of them visible to the eyes with which we pursue our affairs (and what are our affairs?) we barely credit the ritual disavowal—'never any procession no nor journey no never any Pim no nor Bem no never anyone no but me no answer but me yes . . .'—and barely notice how cunningly it does not disavow. Yes, yes, I am mistaken, I am mistaken, said B. in the same way, to placate D. These books do not undo the world; it will be here tomorrow" (p. 206).

17 How seductive in this regard is the possible source for Beckett's "metaphor" which Germaine Brée found in Rabelais. I quote her translation of the passage: [Bacbuc to Panurge] "You say in your world that 'sac' is a word common to all languages and naturally and rightly understandable to all nations, for according to Aesopus all humans are born, a sack around the neck, puny by nature, and perpetually begging one from another" ("Beckett's Abstractors of Quintessence," *French Review*, 36 [1963], 567).

18 Beckett *Imagination Dead Imagine* (London: Calder and Boyars, 1965); translated by the author from *Imagination morte imaginez* (Paris: Éditions de Minuit, 1965).

19 Beckett, quoted in Driver, "Beckett by the Madeleine," p. 23.

20 Beckett, *Le Dépeupleur* (Paris: Éditions de Minuit, 1970).

21 Beckett, *Watt* (New York: Grove Press, 1959), p. 175.

22 Beckett, *Come and Go* (London: Calder and Boyars, 1967), p. 8.

23 Alec Reid, *All I Can Manage, More Than I Could: An Approach to the Plays of Samuel Beckett* (Dublin: Dolmen Press, 1968), pp. 19–20.

24 Driver, "Beckett by the Madeleine," p. 23.

Bibliographical Note

BY FAR THE most extensive bibliography of works by and about Beckett is Raymond Federman's and John Fletcher's *Samuel Beckett: His Works and His Critics* (Berkeley and Los Angeles: University of California Press, 1970). This is a monumental piece of work that takes the reader up to 1968 on Beckett's works and up to 1966 on the criticism. For a compact working bibliography of criticism up to 1968, the reader is referred to Jackson R. Bryer's "Samuel Beckett: A Checklist of Criticism" in Melvin J. Friedman, ed., *Samuel Beckett Now: Critical Approaches to His Novels, Poetry, and Plays* (Chicago: University of Chicago Press, 1970), pp. 219–259.

Index